"Can you talk too much about Christ? Michael Reeves argues 'no!' This book calls us to rejoice in the One in whom is found all joy. No small Jesus here; Jesus writ large and made much of. Enjoy this book, and enjoy the Christ to whom this book points."

Josh Moody, pastor of College Church, Wheaton, Illinois

"God created us 'to glorify and enjoy him forever.' But what does it mean to enjoy God? Michael Reeves has a knack not only for making great truths accessible, but for leading us to bask in the warmth of Christ. Our mediator not only in salvation, but in creation and the consummation, Christ isn't just a gift-giver—he is the Gift. As an example of devotional theology, this book stands out. If you want to love Christ more, you need a better view of him. *Rejoicing in Christ* gives you a front-row seat."

Michael Horton, J. Gresham Machen Professor of Theology, Westminster Seminary California

"Michael Reeves has written a simple and yet elegant introduction to the work of Jesus Christ. He provides a wonderful overview of Jesus in eternity, Jesus triumphing over evil and Jesus reigning forever. Reeves shows that for believers, our life is from Christ, and Christ is our life! His account of Christian doctrine about Jesus is complemented with a treasure trove of historical artwork depicting Jesus, stimulating the mind as well as the heart."

Michael F. Bird, lecturer in theology at Ridley, Melbourne, Australia

"Reeves has expounded a crucial and central doctrine of the gospel with clarity and verve. This is a scintillating treatment of a vital subject."

Robert Letham, lecturer in systematic theology, Wales Evangelical School of Theology

"Mike Reeves has done it again. This is another rich, deep, simple, joyful, thrilling book—theology that does what theology should, pointing us to Jesus, marveling and celebrating."

Andrew Wilson, elder at Kings Church, Eastbourne, and author of several books, including *If God Then What? Wondering Aloud About Truth, Origins & Redemption*

"This is how to write Christology: biblical, theological, historical, pastoral and spiritual! Theology at its best from one of today's best theologians."

Simon Ponsonby, pastor of theology, St Aldate's Church, Oxford

REJOICING IN
CHRIST

Michael Reeves

IVP Academic
An imprint of InterVarsity Press
Downers Grove, Illinois

InterVarsity Press
P.O. Box 1400, Downers Grove, IL 60515-1426
ivpress.com
email@ivpress.com

InterVarsity Press® is the book-publishing division of InterVarsity Christian Fellowship/USA®, a
movement of students and faculty active on campus at hundreds of universities, colleges and schools of
nursing in the United States of America, and a member movement of the International Fellowship of
Evangelical Students. For information about local and regional activities, visit intervarsity.org.

Cover design: Cindy Kiple
Interior design: Beth McGill
Images: © Pattie Calfy/iStockphoto

ISBN 978-0-8308-4022-9 (print)
ISBN 978-0-8308-9819-0 (digital)

Printed in the United States of America ∞

 As a member of the Green Press Initiative, InterVarsity Press is committed to protecting
the environment and to the responsible use of natural resources. To learn more, visit
greenpressinitiative.org.

Library of Congress Cataloging-in-Publication Data

Reeves, Michael (Michael D.)
  Rejoicing in Christ / Michael Reeves.
    pages cm
  "Originally published in the United Kingdom as Christ our
life"—Title page verso.
  Includes bibliographical references and index.
  ISBN 978-0-8308-4022-9 (pbk. : alk. paper)—ISBN 978-0-8308-9819-0
(digital)
  1. Jesus Christ—Person and offices. 2. Christian life. I. Title.
BT203.R44 2015
232—DC23

                                                            2014044450

| P | 19 | 18 | 17 | 16 | 15 | 14 | 13 | 12 | 11 | 10 | 9 | 8 | 7 | 6 | 5 | 4 | 3 |
| Y | 31 | 30 | 29 | 28 | 27 | 26 | 25 | 24 | 23 | 22 | 21 | 20 | 19 | 18 | 17 | 16 |

For my much-loved brother, who bears the name of Christ

If then you have been raised with Christ, seek the things that are above, where Christ is, seated at the right hand of God. Set your minds on things that are above, not on things that are on earth. For you have died, and your life is hidden with Christ in God. When Christ who is your life appears, then you also will appear with him in glory.

COLOSSIANS 3:1-4 ESV

CONTENTS

Introduction: Christianity *Is* Christ   9

1 In the Beginning   13

2 Behold the Man!   33

3 There and Back Again   57

4 Life in Christ   83

5 Come, Lord Jesus!   105

Conclusion: No Other Name Under Heaven   121

Notes   125

Image Credits   129

Scripture Index   133

Christianity *Is* Christ

Jesus Christ, God's perfect Son, is the Beloved of the Father, the Song of the angels, the Logic of creation, the great Mystery of godliness, the bottomless Spring of life, comfort and joy. We were made to find our satisfaction, our heart's rest, in him. Quite simply, this book will be about enjoying him, reveling in his all-sufficiency for us, and considering all that he is: how he reveals such an unexpectedly kind God, how he makes, defines—how he *is*—the good news, and how he not only gives shape to but *is himself* the shape of the Christian life.

Once upon a time a book like this would have been utterly run-of-the-mill. Among the old Puritans, for example, you can scarcely find a writer who did not write—or a preacher who did not preach—something called *The Unsearchable Riches of Christ*, *Christ Set Forth*, *The Glory of Christ* or the like. Yet today, what sells? What puts the smile on the bookseller's face? The book that is about the reader. People want to read about themselves. There's nothing necessarily wrong in that, of course; but that is not primarily what life is about. "For to me, to live is Christ," said the apostle Paul. "What is more, I consider everything a loss because of the surpassing worth of knowing Christ Jesus my Lord" (Phil 1:21; 3:8). Startling words, all too easily dismissed as religious overexcitement. But Paul was not raving; he was speaking plainly the deepest wisdom: that life is found in Jesus Christ, the author and source of it, and if we know him rightly, we will find nothing so desirable, so delightful, as him.

It's not just our self-focus, though; we naturally gravitate, it seems, toward *anything* but Jesus—and Christians almost as much as anyone—whether it's "the Christian worldview," "grace," "the Bible" or "the gospel," as if they were things *in themselves* that could save us. Even "the cross" can get abstracted from Jesus, as if the wood had some power of its own. Other things, wonderful things, vital concepts, beautiful discoveries so easily edge *Jesus* aside. Precious theological concepts meant to describe *him* and *his* work get treated as things in their own right. He becomes just another brick in the wall. But the center, the cornerstone, the jewel in the crown of Christianity is not an idea, a system or a thing; it is not even "the gospel" as such. It is Jesus Christ.

He is not a mere topic, a subject we can pick out from a menu of options. Without him, our gospel or our system—however co-herent, "grace-filled" or "Bible-based"—simply is not Christian. It will only be Christian to the extent that it is about *him*, and then what we make of him will govern what we mean by the word *gospel*. I'm going to dare to say, in fact, that most of our Christian problems and errors of thought come about precisely through forgetting or marginalizing Christ. That is, that despite all our apparent Christian-ness, we fail to build our lives and thoughts upon the Rock. Amid all the debates and disagreements of the Reformation, that was just what the Reformer John Calvin thought:

> For how comes it that we are *carried about with so many strange doctrines*, (Hebrews 13:9) but because the excellence of Christ is not perceived by us? For Christ alone makes all other things suddenly vanish. Hence there is nothing that Satan so much endeavours to accomplish as to bring on mists with the view of obscuring Christ, because he knows, that by this means the

way is opened up for every kind of falsehood. This, therefore, is the only means of retaining, as well as restoring pure doctrine—to place Christ before the view such as he is with all his blessings, that his excellence may be truly perceived.[1]

This book, then, aims for something deeper than a new technique or a call to action: to consider Christ, that he might become more central for you, that you might know him better, treasure him more and enter into his joy. That, happily, is just how we will most honor the Father: by sharing his own everlasting delight in his Son (Jn 5:23). It is also the secret of how to become like the Lord of love (2 Cor 3:18). And as we consider him, we will look at how he *is* our life: our righteousness, our holiness, our hope.

So what do I want from these pages? I can't put it any better than the Scottish preacher Robert Murray M'Cheyne, who wrote to a friend with this advice:

> Learn much of the Lord Jesus. For every look at yourself, take ten looks at Christ. He is altogether lovely. Such infinite majesty, and yet such meekness and grace, and all for sinners, even the chief. Live much in the smiles of God. Bask in His beams. Feel His all-seeing eye settled on you in love, and repose in His almighty arms. . . . Let your soul be filled with a heart-ravishing sense of the sweetness and excellency of Christ and all that is in Him.[2]

Yes! That's what we're about now.

1

In the Beginning

Behind the Curtain

What is it like in eternity? What's there? For millennia, the human imagination has groped and guessed, peering into the darkness. And in that darkness it has dreamed of dreadful gods and goddesses, of devils and powers, or of space and ultimate nothingness. Staggered by immensity, we are left terrified of what might be. If there is a God behind it all, what is he like?

Jesus. That is the Christian answer. He is like Jesus Christ. "In the beginning was the Word," says John 1:1, "and the Word was with God, and the Word was God." Before all other things, before anything else existed, there was God, and there was his Word, who was God. And with that little sentence, a revolution has just happened. Want to see how? Let's see what John means when he writes about "the Word."

In the Old Testament, the Word appears in Genesis 1, as God speaks creation into being (and, given his light-and-darkness language and the big hint "In the beginning," John clearly had Genesis 1 in mind when he was writing). The Word is how God expresses himself. The Word also came to prophets (Is 38:4), was sent to heal and rescue (Ps 107:20) and made known the mind of the LORD (Amos 3:1). But John also had something else from the Old Testament on his mind as he wrote: the tabernacle, the tent where the LORD would come and be with his people in the wilderness, and where his glory would be seen. For when John says that the Word "made his dwelling among us" (Jn 1:14), he puts it strangely: more literally, he writes that the Word "pitched his tent among us."

Now in the innermost part of the tabernacle, the back room, was the Holy of Holies, where the Lord was said to sit "enthroned between the cherubim" on the ark of the covenant

"The law was given through Moses; grace and truth came through Jesus Christ" (Jn 1:17). Christ as the true Word, the true Manna, the true blossoming staff, *Speculum Humanae Salvationis*, c. 1360

(1 Sam 4:4; Lev 16:2). And inside that gold-plated ark were kept the two tablets on which were written the ten "words" or commandments: the law; *the word of God.* For the Israelites, it modeled the truth that the Word of God belongs in the presence—in the very throne!—of God.

The Word of God, then, is the one who belongs in the deepest closeness with God, and the one who displays the innermost reality of who God is. He is "the radiance of God's glory and the exact representation of his being" (Heb 1:3). For he is himself God. He is God's "Amen, the faithful and true witness, the ruler of God's creation" (Rev 3:14).

Here, then, is the revolution: for all our dreams, our dark and frightened imaginings of God, *there is no God in heaven who is unlike Jesus.* For he *is* God. "Anyone who has seen me has seen the Father," he says, for "I and the Father are one" (Jn 14:9; 10:30). God cannot be otherwise.

This was the subject of what was perhaps the greatest battle the church fought in the centuries after the New Testament: to uphold belief that Jesus truly is God, none other than the LORD God of Israel himself. He is, as was enshrined in the stirring words of the

Nicene Creed, "God from God, light from light, true God from true God, begotten not made, of one being with the Father." And no wonder they loved this truth, for through it the sunshine bursts in upon our thoughts of who God is, and what all reality is about: *there is no God in heaven who is unlike Jesus.* Capturing that happy spirit of the Creed, T. F. Torrance was drawn to be quite lyrical as he wrote:

> There is in fact no God behind the back of Jesus, no act of God other than the act of Jesus, no God but the God we see and meet in him. Jesus Christ is the open heart of God, the very love and life of God poured out to redeem humankind, the mighty hand and power of God stretched out to heal and save sinners. All things are in God's hands, but the hands of God and the hands of Jesus, in life and in death, are the same.[1]

Let us then be rid of that horrid, sly idea that behind Jesus, the friend of sinners, there is some more sinister being, one thinner on compassion and grace. There cannot be! Jesus is the Word. He is one with his Father. He is the radiance, the glow, the glory of who his Father is. If God is like Jesus, then, though I am sinful like the dying thief, I can dare to cry, "Remember me" (see Lk 23:42). I know how he will respond. Though I am so spiritually lame and leprous, I can call out to him. For I know just what he is like toward the weak and sick.

In him we see the true meaning of the love, the power, the wisdom, the justice and the majesty of God. As we look through this book at Jesus, then, we will not be looking at someone other than God; we will be contemplating God himself. And in fact, if we do *not* go to this Word to know God, then all our thoughts about God, however respectful, worshipful or philosophically satisfying, will be nothing but idolatry.

An old Puritan preacher Stephen Charnock once wrote:

> Is not God the Father of lights, the supreme truth, the most delectable object. . . . Is he not light without darkness, love without unkindness, goodness without evil, purity without filth, all excellency to please, without a spot to distaste? Are

not all other things infinitely short of him, more below him than a cab of dung is below the glory of the sun?[2]

Talk about an enviable delight! Here was a man for whom the very thought of God brought rhapsodies of joy. In that outburst we hear a man who seems to carry the sunshine with him, a man with a core of comfort. So how could he be so besotted? Whence such gladness in God? Charnock could not have been plainer: true knowledge of the living God is found in and through Christ. But what we see in Christ is so beautiful it can make the sad sing for joy and the dead spring to life:

> Nothing of God looks terrible in Christ to a believer. The sun is risen, shadows are vanished, God walks upon the battlements of love, justice hath left its sting in a Saviour's side, the law is disarmed, weapons out of his hand, his bosom open, his bowels yearn, his heart pants, sweetness and love is in all his carriage. And this is life eternal, to know God believingly in the glories of his mercy and justice in Jesus Christ.[3]

In Christ the Word, we exchange darkness for light as we think of God. For he perfectly shows us an unsurpassably desirable God, a kind God who is against all that is wrong, a God who thaws us. And only when we see that will we truly love him. Martin Luther said that "we were totally unable to come to a recognition of the Father's favor and grace except through the Lord Christ, who is the mirroring image of the Father's heart. Without Christ we see nothing in God but an angry and terrible Judge."[4]

If we are to be drawn from jaded, anxious thoughts of God, we need such a knowledge of Christ. Every day. Not of "God" undefined, but of Christ the Word, the one in whom all the perfections of the living God shine so brightly. Take it away, Richard Sibbes:

> What makes his power sweet to his children? and his justice, in confounding their enemies, and giving rewards? and his

wisdom sweet, in reconciling justice and mercy together wisely in Christ? All that makes this so lovely, is his grace and love. . . . So that if we would see the glory of God, it appears most in grace, and mercy, and lovingkindness, and such sweet attributes. This makes all things in God amiable; for now we can think of his justice, and not fear. It is fully satisfied in Christ. We can think of his power with comfort. It serves for our good to subdue all our enemies. There is no attribute, though it be terrible in itself, but it is sweet and amiable, because God looks graciously on us in his beloved. . . . We must take God, not as considered abstractively and simply, but God in Christ; for other notions of God are terrible.[5]

You Who Sit Enthroned Between the Cherubim, Shine Forth

The very fact that God has this Word tells us something extraordinary and delightful about him. For it is not simply that here is a God who *happens* to speak (any old god can do that): no, it is *of the very nature* of this God to have a Word to speak. God cannot be Word-less, for the Word *is* God. Here then is a God who could never be anything but communicative, expansive, outgoing. Since God cannot be without this Word, he simply could not ever be reclusive. For eternity this Word sounds out, telling us of an uncontainable God of exuberance and abundance, an overflowing God of surplus, a glorious God of grace.

"But wait," cry the critics ("for such men, I regret to say, do exist"),[6] "is this really so revolutionary? Take Allah, for example: does he not also have a word, the Qur'an?" Ah, but what a difference! Allah has *a book*—but he could do without it; it does not imply for a moment that he has the same abounding nature as the God of Jesus. This book of his tells us *what* Allah wants from us, and it tells us *about* Allah and the character he claims for himself. But that is not at all what we mean when we speak of Jesus as the Word of God. Where the Qur'an speaks *about* God, Jesus *is* God. He does not merely unveil some truth for us, some other principle or system of thought. Like light going out from its source, this Word actually brings God to us. In him, a direct encounter with God happens. The difference is stark: the Word who *is* God reveals a God of innate grace, and he does not just hand down information that we might know *about* God; in him, God delights to meet with us and be with us.

"This Is My Son!"

As well as being God's eternal Word, Jesus is also God's eternal Son—and you can already feel the difference in what that means. "Word" is a title that speaks more of his *oneness* with God, the fact that he *is* God; "Son" brings out the other sweet truth, that he has a real *relationship* with God.

Actually, "relationship" is putting it mildly: the Father loves his Son with a unique and quite dazzling intensity. He did so from before the foundation of the world (Jn 17:24), and now he rejoices to let all the world hear "This is my beloved Son, in whom I am well pleased" (Mt 3:17 KJV). For the Son is "the One he loves" (Eph 1:6), "my chosen one in whom I delight" (Is 42:1), the one he yearns to glorify. As such, the Son is the one for whom he does everything, his Alpha and Omega: all things would be created for him, the heir (Col 1:16).

Sons are often said to be "chips off the old block," and in the Bible especially, a true son was expected to be like his father, in his image and likeness as Seth was the image and likeness of Adam (Gen 5:3). Jesus told the Jews in his day, "If you were Abraham's children, . . . then you would do the things Abraham did" (Jn 8:39), and said that peacemakers can be called "children of God" because of how they are like God the peacemaker (Mt 5:9; see also Lk 6:35-36). But before and above them all, Jesus is the Son of God, for without one whit of distortion he is *precisely* like his Father.

The image. The heir. The beloved. As the fourth-century theologian Athanasius put it: "The Son is the Father's *All*."[7]

HO! HO! HOMOOUSIOS!

Before the mushy tales of Santa's sleigh and his sack of presents got going, the stories told about St. Nick were rather different. The one Christian mothers loved to use to comfort their little ones was of the venerable bishop, not shaking his belly like a bowlful of jelly, but rosy-cheeked with ire, smiting the arch-heretic Arius at the Council of Nicea.

St. Nicholas the Wonderworker's legendary Christmas punch

For some years, Arius had been broadcasting his belief that the Son was not eternal, God himself; the Son was instead a created thing, made by God to go and fashion a universe. Alarmed by the division this teaching caused, the newly converted Roman emperor Constantine called for a council of bishops to discuss the matter at Nicaea in A.D. 325. It was there, they said, that Nicholas of Myra heard Arius for himself; and there, unable to contain his anger at such blasphemy, he let fly.

To be fair, Arius and his followers did seek to have biblical arguments. They would turn to Hebrews 1:5, for example, which quotes Psalm 2, where God says, "You are my Son; *today* I have become your Father,"[8] and they'd ask, "What about the day before, *before* God became his Father? He can't have been the Son then." Clever, eh? Of course, it was simply tearing a sentence out of context to make it say what they wanted. In Acts 13:32-34, Paul quotes the very same words as referring to Jesus' resurrection (and elsewhere backs up the thought, arguing that Jesus "was appointed the Son of God in power *by his resurrection*" [Rom 1:4]). Now if Hebrews 1:5 means there was a time before he was the Son, then Acts 13:33 must mean that that time was before the resurrection: before then he was not the Son. But

God could hardly have made it clearer that Jesus *was* his Son before the resurrection: he announced it as publicly as could be, calling Jesus his beloved Son at both his baptism and the transfiguration. Indeed, he was the Son before he was born of Mary, else how could it be said that "God sent his Son" into the world (Gal 4:4; Rom 8:3; Jn 3:17)? What we will see later on is that God's words to his Son— "*today* I have become your Father"—so far from being a cause for Christian worry, are cause for the most staggering joy.

Why, then, did Nick and the other opponents of Arius react to his teaching with such adrenaline-pumped fury? Contrary to the claims of the energetic Christianity-has-been-nothing-but-a-history-of-irascible-bigots movement, it was not because they were narrow-minded morons. With impressive perception, they saw that Arius was throwing away the God of love and the gospel of grace in exchange for a steely idol who lacked any real conception of kindness.

According to Arius, God had created the Son so as to do the hard graft of dealing with the universe for him. Fair enough, but that said something profound: it was not that the Father truly *loved* the Son; the Son was just his hired workman. And if the Bible ever spoke of the Father's pleasure in the Son, it can only have been because the Son had done a good job. That, presumably, is how to get in with the God who is simply the Employer. But that is no fatherly God of true relationships and heartfelt kindness.

Actually, Arius's view had yet more worrying connotations: if God is not inherently and eternally loving, what moves us who are made in his image? Not love for his Son, if even he lacks that. Perhaps we just need to do the right things and make the right choices. Well, we can do that easily enough without much help. No need for a new birth and a new heart with the god of Arius, it would seem.

Thus the Christian church gathered together at Nicaea and agreed forever to confess that the Son is "of one being [*homoousios*] with the Father." God isn't using him as hired help, and he isn't using

God to get heavenly glory. He has *always* been at the Father's side. He is the *eternally beloved*, the one who shows that there is a most loving Father in heaven, the one who can share with us more than a business understanding with God: sonship!

Who He Is Changes the Gospel

Even for Christians, overlooking Jesus is easier than falling off a log, it seems. We instinctively think of God, life, grace, reality with rarely a pause to have Jesus shape what we mean by those things. We can even have a "Christian worldview" and find Jesus is but an interesting feature in its landscape; we can even have a "gospel" and find Jesus is just the delivery boy who brings home the *real* goods, whether that be salvation, heaven or whatever. But that must change if we are to take seriously the fact that he is the beloved Son.

First, if there is nothing more precious to the Father than him, there cannot be any blessing higher than him or anything better than him. In every way, he himself *must be* the "very great reward" of the gospel (Gen 15:1). He is the treasure of the Father, shared with us. Sometimes we find ourselves tiring of Jesus, stupidly imagining that we have seen all there is to see and used up all the pleasure there is to be had in him. We get spiritually bored. But Jesus has satisfied the mind and heart of the infinite God for eternity. Our boredom is simple blindness. If the Father can be infinitely and eternally satisfied in him, then he must be overwhelmingly all-sufficient for us. In every situation, for eternity.

Second, his sonship—his relationship with his Father—is the gospel and salvation he has to share with us. That is *his* joy. As the Father shares his Son with us, so the Son shares his relationship with the Father. That is why in Matthew 11:27-30 Jesus *first* says, "No one knows the Son except the Father, and no one knows the Father except the Son and those to whom the Son chooses to reveal him"

(v. 27), and *then* says, "Come to me, all you who are weary and burdened, and I will give you rest. Take my yoke upon you and learn from me, for I am gentle and humble in heart, and you will find rest for your souls. For my yoke is easy and my burden is light" (vv. 28-30). For his relationship with his Father shapes the rest, yoke and

burden he has to offer. In fact, his relationship with his Father *is* the rest, yoke and burden he has to offer. To know the Father, to be humble before him and gentle like him: that is the rest we all seek, the only yoke that is easy, the only burden that is light. And as Samuel Rutherford put it, those who take it shall "find it such a burden as wings unto a bird, or sails to a ship."[9]

The Heavenly Rose, 1892. Gustave Doré's illustration of Dante's vision at the end of *Divine Comedy*, where God's love is described as a blossoming flower of light.

The Love Which Moves the Sun

For eternity, the Word was spoken out, telling of a God of overflowing life. For eternity, the Son was cherished, telling of a God of bottomless love. Given that this is the God we meet in Jesus, perhaps it is unsurprising that he should decide to have a creation, to unfold and spread his life and love. The eighteenth-century preacher Jonathan Edwards put it unforgettably:

> The creation of the world seems to have been especially for this end, that the eternal Son of God might obtain a spouse, toward whom he might fully exercise the infinite benevolence of his nature, and to whom he might, as it were, open

TRINITY OR JESUS?

Some authors will tell you that "*the Trinity* is the governing center of all Christian belief";[10] some will say things like, "The center, the cornerstone, the jewel in the crown of Christianity . . . is *Jesus Christ*."[11] Different writers, different emphases? Muddle-headed Christians?

No, there is no contradiction or confusion here: to honor Jesus is to honor the triune God. For if we are to speak of Jesus, we must speak of him as the *Son* of God, as the Word who makes his *Father* known; we must speak of him as the Christ ("the anointed one"), the one anointed with the *Holy Spirit*. In other words, in speaking of Jesus, we cannot but speak of the Trinity. For he is the one who makes known the triune God. The Trinity, then, is not some complex add-on to Jesus, a higher-level matter for those ready to go beyond simple trust in him: in thinking about the Trinity we are pressing in to know Jesus better.

And on the other hand, if we are to speak of the Trinity, we must speak of the Father who is made known by his Son Jesus Christ in the power of the Spirit. Any "trinity" that can shuffle off, untethered to Jesus, is nothing but a philosophical party game. You can find such trinities bobbing around out there, filled with excited talk of love, relationship and the great conga that is Father, Son and Spirit. But detached from Jesus, they become only heavenly boogies shaped by each person's own dance preference (something that puts the fear of God into those who prefer a quiet sit down). No, *Jesus* is the one who makes known the triune God, who shows us the love of God and the life of God. To be truly trinitarian we must be constantly Christ-centered.

and pour forth all that immense fountain of condescension, love and grace that was in his heart, and that in this way God might be glorified.[12]

And so, as God's outgoing Word, as the Son filled to bursting with his Father's love, he became the Logic behind the creation, "the beginning," the foundation of it all—and the one it would all be for (Col 1:17-18). Then, in the power of the Spirit who hovered over the waters, the Word went out. God spoke, and through that potent Word all things came into being. As the Father said of the Son, "In the beginning, Lord, you laid the foundations of the earth, and the heavens are the work of your hands" (Heb 1:10; citing Ps 102:25). The Son became in fact the firstborn over all creation (Col 1:15).

Sadly, so many Christians have a background virus in their understanding of the gospel here. It's not easy to spot, but it eats away at all their confidence in Christ. It's this: the sneaking suspicion that while Jesus is a savior, he's not really the Creator of all. So they sing of his love on a Sunday—and *there* it is true—but walking home through the streets, past the people and the places where Real Life goes on, they don't feel it is *Christ's* world. As if the universe is a neutral place. As if Christianity is just something we have smeared on top of Real Life. Jesus is reduced to being little more than a comforting nibble of spiritual chocolate, an imaginary friend who "saves souls" but not much else.

The Bible knows of no such piffling and laughable Christlet. "Through him all things were made; without him nothing was made that has been made" (Jn 1:3). As such, it is farcical to imagine that he, the Creator, the one above and before all things, should be about no more than "saving souls." The Lord of the cosmos will have a cosmic purpose: to renew his entire world, destroying evil from it forever.

Since Jesus Christ is the one "through whom all things came" (1 Cor 8:6), God's agent of creation who continues to uphold and sustain the creation he brought into being, the marks of his artistry are all round us. From the tiniest sea urchin to the brightest star, all things bear his magnificent stamp. The heavens cannot but declare his glory, for they are his craftsmanship, and they continue to hold together only in him. His character is written into the grain of the universe so intimately that even to think against Christ the Logos you must think against logic and descend into folly (Ps 14:1). In his world, our faculties work better the more they are harnessed to faith in him. Then we are able to be more logical, more vibrant, more imaginative, more creative, for we are working with the grain.

Someone who took this very seriously was Jonathan Edwards. Since God had created in order to communicate himself, Edwards believed that the universe is "full of images of divine things, as full as a language is of words."[13] The tiniest details in everything, from spiders and silkworms to rainbows and roses, all pour forth knowledge about Christ and his ways. For example, the "rising and setting of the sun is a type [a picture] of the death and resurrection of Christ," the true light of the world.[14] "Milk, by its whiteness, represents the purity of the Word of God. It fitly represents the Word because of its sweetness and nourishing nature, and being for the saints in this present state wherein they are children."[15]

This, said the Reformer Martin Luther, was why in Genesis 2:1 the heavens and the earth are said to be filled with a "host" (or "army") of creatures, for "God created all these creatures to be in active military service, to fight for us continually against the devil."[16] That is, they reflect the truth with which to beat the lies of the accuser: through the sun freely driving away the darkness every morning, we can reflect on the grace, beauty and victory of Christ; through drinking water we sense how he refreshes the thirsty; through how freely we breathe the air we experience his openhandedness, and so on.

Echoes of an Ancient Song

There is an old Victorian argument that Christianity is little more than recycled paganism, its best ideas simply stolen and rehashed.

"THERE, BUT FOR THE GRACE OF GOD, GO I"

"There, but for the grace of God, go I." So said the English
Reformer John Bradford, apparently, when he saw prisoners
being taken for execution. Death, he knew, was what his sin
deserved. He would in the end be executed himself, though
not for any sin. In 1555, he was burned to death at Smithfield,
London, as part of "Bloody" Queen Mary's campaign against
the evangelicals. Tied to the stake, he turned to his fellow
martyr, John Leaf, and said, "Be of good comfort, brother; for
we shall have a merry supper with the Lord this night."

Most Christians take mealtimes as a chance to thank
God and remember him as their provider, but Bradford saw
every part of the day as a gospel reminder. When waking
in the morning, he would "call to mind the great joy and
blessedness of the everlasting resurrection . . . that most
clear light and bright morning . . . after the long darkness."
Seeing the sun, he would praise the Light of the world. Rising, he would think on how Christ raises us up. Dressing,
he would pray, "O Christ, clothe me with thine own self"
and remember "how we are incorporated into Christ . . .
how he clothes us." Eating meat, he would compare it to
feeding on the body of Christ. When returning to his home
he would think "how joyful a return, it will be to come to
our eternal, most quiet, and most happy home." And when
finally undressing and getting into bed at night, he would
think of putting "off the old man, with his lusts" and ready-
ing himself for the sleep of death: "As you are not afraid to
enter into your bed, and to dispose yourself to sleep; so be
not afraid to die."[17]

For Bradford, this is Christ's world, and we live most
happily in it when we acknowledge that constantly.

After all, wrote many an excited anthropologist, sensing blood: ancient Egypt, Greece and Rome knew of virgin births, and of dying and rising gods. Orpheus, descending to Hades to rescue his bride; Bacchus, the god born of woman, honored through wine; Osiris, the "resurrected" god: do these not all sound familiar—all too similar, in fact, to Jesus?

C. S. Lewis adored such myths, and in his youth was haunted by the story of Balder, the tragically slain Norse god of light and joy. After Lewis's conversion to Christianity, he came to view these resemblances as anything but problematic. For, given that this is Christ's world, *of course* the stories we tell and the dreams we weave echo him. He defines ultimate reality, and we simply do not have the ability to fashion any real alternative. We can imagine whole new worlds, but those worlds will not be wholly new. To seem real at all they must partake of some reality, and that is defined by Christ the Creator. Thus our stories are filled with serpent-like villains, with tragedies and damsels in distress, with brave young heroes who struggle against the darkness, who are wounded in the fight, who win, who finally get the girl and live happily ever after. For that is the story of Christ.

Balder the Beautiful

When Lewis read Homer and saw his idea that only a drink of sacrificial blood can restore a ghost to rationality, he saw it as "one of the most striking among many *pagan anticipations of the truth*."[18]

He turns to a passage in Plato's *Republic*, where Plato

> asks us therefore to imagine a perfectly righteous man treated
> by all around him as a monster of wickedness. We must
> picture him, still perfect, while he is bound, scourged, and
> finally impaled (the Persian equivalent of crucifixion). At this
> passage a Christian reader starts and rubs his eyes. What is
> happening? Yet another of these lucky coincidences? But
> presently he sees that there is something here which cannot
> be called luck at all.[19]

Far from it. Or take Virgil's *Fourth Eclogue*, which, though written
decades before the birth of Jesus, speaks uncannily of the birth of a
child from heaven who will usher in a new and golden age. Lewis
made this a regular part of his Christmas reading. Myths could be
enjoyed and not feared. For it is not that Christianity and the myths
together represent something *more primeval than themselves*, showing
Christianity to be just one more human dream. That was what the
Victorian anthropologists had argued: that all the dying and rising
gods were *really* about the passage of the seasons, through the death
of winter to the new life of spring. Instead, it is the passage of the
seasons from death to life that represents what is more fundamental:
their death-defeating Creator. Beautifully, it means that, as G. K.
Chesterton put it, Christianity meets

> the mythological search for romance by being a story and the
> philosophical search for truth by being a true story. That is
> why the ideal figure had to be a historical character as nobody
> had ever felt Adonis or Pan to be a historical character. But
> that is also why the historical character had to be the ideal
> figure; and even fulfill many of the functions given to these
> other ideal figures; why he was at once the sacrifice and the
> feast, why he could be shown under the emblems of the
> growing vine or the rising sun.[20]

The God of Abraham, Isaac and Jacob

On the sixth and last day of Genesis 1, God's Word went out for the last time in creation. "God said, 'Let us make man in our image'" (Gen 1:26). But then what? What was the Word now to do with himself? For sure, there was now a universe to uphold, but he would never be about sustaining the universe *for its own sake*, and it would be a long time before he would be in that manger in Bethlehem. Yet he is God's Word; he could never be inactive. It is through him that God would speak to the humanity he had created. His Father would not act without him, and he seemed positively impatient to be with his people.

Right after John introduced the Word at the beginning of his Gospel, he wrote that "No one has ever seen God" (Jn 1:18). Had he left it there, his Gospel would have been laughed out of every synagogue, for you don't have to read the Old Testament very carefully to see that thousands *did* see God. Jacob, after wrestling with him, exclaimed, "I saw God face to face" (Gen 32:30); we read that the Lord would regularly speak with Moses "face to face, as a man speaks with his friend" (Ex 33:11), and at Sinai, with his brother Aaron, his nephews and seventy elders of Israel, he "saw the God of Israel" (Ex 24:10); Samson's parents cried, "We have seen God!" (Judg 13:22), as did Isaiah, who wailed, "Woe to me! . . . [M]y eyes have seen the King, the LORD Almighty" (Is 6:5). Sometimes the sight

Der Prophet Hesekiel.

Christ as the Glory of the Lord in Ezekiel 1, by Lucas Cranach the Younger, Wittenberg Bible, 1541

was described as seeing "the glory of the LORD," as when Ezekiel "got up and went out to the plain. And the glory of the LORD was standing there" (Ezek 3:23). And this sight of the glory of the LORD "appeared to *all the people*" of Israel in the exodus, a people who numbered many hundreds of thousands (Lev 9:23; Ex 16:10).

It was important, then, that John went on: "No one has ever seen God, *but God the One and Only, who is at the Father's side, has made him known*" (Jn 1:18 NIV 1984). Who had they all been seeing? Not God the Father but God the One and Only: the Word, the Son, the Glory of God. Sometimes in the Old Testament he is referred to as "the Angel of the LORD," who is not a created angel ("messenger") but who, while sent as a messenger from the Lord, is clearly God himself. The angel of the Lord speaks as Lord and God, and is addressed as such (Gen 16:10-13; Ex 3:2-15); Jacob blesses in his name, calling him his God and deliverer (Gen 48:15-16); and he is said to be the one who brings Israel up out of Egypt (Judg 2:1).

Christ expels Adam and Eve from the Garden of Eden,
St. Albans Psalter, c. 1130

Yet it is not as if the Son simply has a walk-on part in the Old Testament, randomly popping up every now and again just to keep us all amused. You can get that impression from the breathlessness with which some speak of the man/God who wrestled with Jacob (Gen 32:24-30), or the fourth man in the fire who joined Shadrach, Meshach and Abednego, the one who looked "like the Son of God" (Dan 3:25 KJV). As if those were unheard of oddities, exceptions to the rule that the God of the Old Testament is really the Father alone (or worse, just some "God in general"). The difficulty with this view is that it tends to treat Jesus as a later, New Testament *appendix* to the "true" God (with the result that we fear what this "true" God behind Jesus is like).

Jesus' own claim for himself, however, was not that he was simply any old divine being or "God"; his claim was that he was quite specifically the Lord God of Israel himself, come in the flesh. "Very truly I tell you, . . . before Abraham was born, *I am*!" he said in John 8:58, pinning to himself the divine name I AM (which we render in English as "the LORD"). Thus it is not an odd thing at all that he should appear, speak to and be with his people. For he is "the LORD" who goes out "from the LORD" (Gen 19:24). He is "the LORD Almighty" who says, "the LORD Almighty has sent me" (Zech 2:8-9). He is the one in whom the faithful have always trusted. As John Calvin put it, "Never did God reveal Himself outside of Christ," and "apart from the Mediator, God never showed favor toward the ancient people, nor ever gave hope of grace to them . . . [so that] the hope of all the godly has ever reposed in Christ alone."[21]

In other words, what was Christ doing "B.C."? He was experiencing what it means—tasting what it would soon mean—to be Savior, King, Prophet, Priest, Sacrifice and all he would be and accomplish. As the Word of the Lord he made God known. He judged evil (Gen 19:24). He saved his people (Is 63:9; Jude 5), guiding them through the wilderness, feeding them with manna and defending them from their enemies. He even had friendly times of fellowship, communing with his people (Gen 18:1-8; Ex 24:10-11): he was after all the bridegroom of his people, and he loved them like the finest husband (Is 62:5).

He also served as a mediator and intercessor, praying for his people as a man pleads for a friend (Job 16:20-21; 1 Sam 2:25). With this, we begin to see him more obviously anticipating what was to come. In a striking scene in Judges, the angel of the Lord appeared to Samson's parents; when they offered a sacrifice, "as the flame blazed up from the altar toward heaven, the angel of the LORD ascended in the flame"—*as if he were the sacrifice* (Judg 13:20). Jonathan Edwards wrote of this:

> Here Christ appeared to Manoah in a representation both of his incarnation and death: of his incarnation in that he appeared in a human form, and of his death and sufferings represented by the sacrifice of this kid, which Christ now signified by ascending up in the flame of the sacrifice—intimating that it was he that was the great sacrifice that must be offered up to God for a sweet savor in the fire of his wrath, as that kid was burned and ascended up in that flame.[22]

And since he was the one who would "appear in the cloud over the atonement cover" in the Holy of Holies (Lev 16:2), we can only imagine how he watched the work of the high priest, how he saw the sprinkled blood of each sacrifice, and how it made him think of the work before him.

See, Your King Comes to You

Yet while he could rescue his people from Egypt, give them bread from heaven and even come to be with them, he wanted more. We needed more. He wanted and we needed what those things all pointed toward: true rescue, bread that gives everlasting life, his presence with us for good. And so that promise was given: "The virgin will conceive and will give birth to a son, and will call him Immanuel" (Is 7:14).

2

Behold the Man!

And the Glory of the Lord Shall Be Revealed

And so it was that the Lord of all creation, the one who must stoop even to look upon the heavens and the earth (Ps 113:6), stooped down from heaven to take the form of a servant. He created his own mother, and then before all the angels the Father sent forth his great Son.

The apostle Paul wrote that Christ Jesus "emptied himself" in taking the form of a servant (Phil 2:7 NRSV), but it shouldn't be thought that he who was in very nature God emptied some *thing* out of himself, somehow un-Goding himself. He did not empty himself *of* anything he was: he emptied *himself*, humbling himself to be God with us in the form of a baby. The One on high became low, the Creator became a creature, the Word became speechless, the very power of God became a helpless fetus.

"Then suddenly the Lord you are seeking will come to his temple," Malachi had prophesied (Mal 3:1); and here he was. How faithful old Simeon must have reeled and gasped that day in the temple when he held this one, his Lord, in his arms (Lk 2:25-35)! For here was the one who belonged in the Holy of Holies. The one high priests trembled to approach was there in the flesh, now with and alongside his people forever. No wonder the world seemed so full of the demon-possessed in those days: all hell had been summoned to take up arms against the great prince of heaven. No wonder the Gospels record so many who were amazed and astonished by him, as if they were witnesses to a volcano: his presence was an apocalypse, a cataclysm, an earth-shaking upheaval of all things. God with us!

Bernard of Clairvaux, known to history as "the honey-flowing doctor" of the twelfth century, adoringly called this event "the kiss of God." For here the Word or mouth of God comes to meet us in love. The bridegroom comes to be one flesh with his bride. Here we see the boundless passion and compassion this Lord has for his people.

ONE LORD JESUS CHRIST

It is rather comforting to know that there have always been screwballs hanging around the church. It's not just today. And

The Body of Abel found by Adam and Eve by William Blake, c. 1826

in the second century, the prize for screwiest of the lot would probably (though the competition was hot) have gone to the Cainites. Believing that creation, what with all its mess and pain, was a truly terrible thing, they held that the god who had come up with the idea must be a complete scoundrel. The real devil, in fact. Thus for them, the true heroes of the Bible were people like Cain, who opposed the wicked Creator. Instead of worshiping that Creator God of the Old Testament, they claimed to worship an entirely different Savior God, one they believed they saw in the New Testament, one who would rescue them out of this creation and take them to a realm of pure spirit.

Orthodox Christians wondered how a God of love could allow such complete rot. For the message of the opening verses of John's Gospel was clear as Austrian crystal: the Savior *was* the Word who was in the beginning with God, through whom all things were made. Not a different being. The Savior was the Creator. Meaning that salvation could never mean salvation *out of* this world. Salvation is not about undoing the work of some other god (the Creator). Instead, the very same Word who went out into the void in creation is the one who went out into the sin-ravaged world in salvation. And coming into his own creation, he came not to undo it but to redeem it. It was, as it were, the first day of a new week of creation, the Word going out once again to bring light into darkness, to create life, to recover what was his (Jn 1:4-5).

Sometimes the church's theologians explained this by telling the story of the Image of God (that is, the story of Christ as the Image of God [Col 1:15; 2 Cor 4:4], who reflects and images his Father so perfectly, having always enjoyed perfect communion with him). It all started when humankind was made in *his* image. We were created to be like him, to know and enjoy communion with God, as he always had, that we might reflect God's graciousness, holiness and beauty. Like him. Yet in Eden, as we turned away from God and trusted the serpent, we became anything but like him: selfish, faithless, attentive to Satan but not God. It is as if humankind was a portrait of Christ, drawn in his likeness, now horribly defaced by sin. But then Christ returns to have his portrait redrawn and renewed—not to commission an entirely new piece of work but to renovate that original. The Image of God would come to show us what it means to be in the image of God, and to remold us into what we were created to be.

"The Pattern of the One to Come"

So why exactly did the Son of God become a man, the son of a woman? Here it helps if we back up for a moment to look at the first man, Adam. Why? First of all, because the first Adam was the "pattern of the one to come" (Rom 5:14), a picture of what Christ, "the last Adam" (1 Cor 15:45), would be like. Adam, for example, was crowned by God as the ruler of all creation: "Rule over the fish of the sea and the birds of the sky and over every living creature that moves on the ground" he was told (Gen 1:28). He was to look after the creation as God's steward and regent. But in all that of course he was serving as a mere illustration of the one to whom every knee will bow, to whom every creature will submit: the last Adam, who would be crowned the everlasting king of all.

Adam was also created "in the image of God" (Gen 1:27), to be like the one who is the bright radiance of his Father's glory. And—

God leads Adam to Eden, Monreale Cathedral. In the history of Christian art, Christ and Adam have frequently been shown as looking alike. Thus Christ is often depicted with red hair to resemble the man (*adam* in Hebrew, a word closely related to *adom*, meaning "red") formed from the red earth (*adamah*).

strikingly—Adam is called "the son of God" in Luke 3:38. For he was created specially to be like *the* Son of God, reveling in the love and care that the eternal Son had always enjoyed. He was made to know the love of the Father. Now Adam undid all that he was made to be by sinning: in listening to Satan he was no longer imaging God; in doubting God's fatherly kindness to him he was no longer being a faithful son. He was the prodigal son. But even in his sin he managed to serve as a *mirror* image of the

Son of God. Adam did not do what God had commanded, precisely because he no longer loved the Father. In that moment he could not have been more perfectly opposite to the Son of God who said, "I love the Father and do exactly what [he] has commanded me" (Jn 14:31).

More than all that, the first Adam shows us what the last Adam is like through his marriage. The account of it in Genesis 2 certainly makes you sit up and wonder. For there, in a world before all death and injury, Adam is wounded. He falls into a deep, strange, death-like sleep, and from his side the Lord takes a rib and builds it into a woman (Gen 2:21-22). She comes from him, and they become one, husband and wife (v. 24). John Calvin wrote that "in this we see a true resemblance of our union with the Son of God."[1] What does this mean? The biblical commentator Matthew Henry elaborates:

> In this (as in many other things) Adam was a figure of him that was to come; for out of the side of Christ, the second Adam, his spouse the church was formed, when he slept the sleep, the deep sleep, of death upon the cross, in order to which his side was opened, and there came out blood and water, blood to purchase his church and water to purify it to himself.[2]

GOOD NEWS FOR THE BRUISED

For too many, *marriage* is a word to wince at. It evokes pain, whether because of unfulfilled longings for marriage or bad experience of it. Even Adam did not model marriage well, standing quietly by as his wife was beguiled by evil, and blaming her when he could, rather than taking the blame for her. But the reason marriage evokes such strong emotions is because of how central it is to all reality. History begins with a marriage in Genesis and it ends with a marriage in Revelation, with "the Holy City, the new Jerusalem, coming down out of heaven from God, prepared as a bride beautifully dressed for her husband" (Rev 21:2). Marriage—*this* marriage—is God's definitive "happily ever after." And that is just why a bad marriage is so painful and upsetting, for it mangles something so tenderly beautiful and good.

We could go further: marriage at its worst always manages to present the relationship between Christ and the church *in photographic negative*. It inverts the ultimate truth about marriage. Take Judges 19, which is probably the darkest chapter in all the Bible. Set at the foul end of Israel's spiritual slide in the book of Judges, it tells a story of chilling viciousness and sexual abuse. An Israelite priest takes his wife to Gibeah (actually she is a concubine: part wife, part property, a "sort of" wife, which reveals that this priest is not quite Prince Charming). The house is surrounded by a mob baying to have sex with *the man*. "So the man took his concubine and sent *her* outside to them, and they raped her and abused throughout the night" (Judg 19:25). And as if that isn't nauseating enough, the next morning when he opens the door and sees her broken body in the doorway, her hands pitifully reached out toward the house, he barks at her, "Get up; let's go." A cold-blooded husband, sacrificing his wife for his own safety: he is the exact reverse of Jesus, who in tender love went out into the darkness to sacrifice himself for his bride, to make her safe.

Christians who flinch at the thought of marriage can thus know two sweet comforts. First, any experience of faithlessness, cruelty or coldness in marriage hurts ultimately because those things are *unlike the* Marriage. They have tasted the opposite of what the church finds in her Bridegroom. Second, all Christians, single or married, find their deepest identity here with him. All our longings for true love and happiness ever after will be gratified to overflow at the wedding supper of the Lamb.

No wonder the apostle Paul, reading of this first wedding in Genesis 2, saw it as a picture of the last and ultimate wedding, saying, "This is a profound mystery—but I am talking about Christ and the church" (Eph 5:32). In Adam we see Christ's glorious intention: to give life to his bride, and to be one with her.

O Adam, What Have You Done?

It is good to look at Adam as the pattern of the one to come, as one who teaches us about the Last Adam. But there is another and more vital reason to look to Adam so as to understand Christ. For Adam is more: he is our natural identity.

In Genesis 5, when Adam has a son, we are told that "he had a son in his own likeness, in his own image" (Gen 5:3). A chip off the old block, in other words. Created to be in the image and likeness of God, Adam had been distinctly *unlike* God, and now the world would be filled with the patter of delinquent feet. Adam became the father of a race *like him*. As Ezra was supposed to have said in one of those obscure books of the Apocrypha: "O Adam, what have you done? For though it was you who sinned, the fall was not yours alone, but ours also who are your descendants" (2 Esdras 7:118 NRSV).

The apostle Paul put it with the bluntness of a hammer:

> sin entered the world *through one man*, and death through sin . . . many died *by the trespass of the one man . . . by the trespass of the one man*, death reigned . . . *one trespass* resulted in the condemnation for all people . . . *through the disobedience of the one man* the many were made sinners. (Rom 5:12, 15, 17-19)

In other words, old John Donne was right: no man is an island. Adam's sin affects us all. Because of Adam, we sin; because of Adam, we die.

Adam as the Root of Humanity by **Hartmann Schedel, 1493**

At this point I can hear the sirens of the thought police come wailing up the street. For this is outrageous talk. Am I not the master of my fate, the captain of my soul? Do I not determine my own destiny? It's hard to hear this in a culture so soused in Hollywood goo, but: no. We have all been born into a problem that goes back to before we did anything, before we even existed: we have all been born of Adam. In his likeness. Of his family, sharing his sinful identity. Instead of being sinners because we each sin, we were born sinners, and *that's* why we sin and die. "As the old saying goes, 'From evildoers come evil deeds'" (1 Sam 24:13). We're just acting out who we are. (Hold on through this dark bit: the light shines so much brighter because of it.)

Actually, I suspect we do all believe this—when it suits us. For what if we really were all islands? What if we came into the world spotless and unaffected by sin? If we only ever suffered and died because of our own personal sin? Well then, what of the boy born mentally handicapped? What of the girl with congenital HIV? Then we'd have to say, "Those poor children are suffering because of *their own* sin." But Paul gets us away from such hard-boiled callousness: we each have a problem that goes deeper than our own birth, all the way back to Adam.

In 1 Corinthians 15, Paul makes a similar point, that "in Adam all die," but there he clothes those simple words with images that gleam.

> Christ has indeed been raised from the dead, the *firstfruits* of those who have fallen asleep. For since death came through a man, the resurrection of the dead comes also through a man. For as in Adam all die, so in Christ all will be made alive. But each in his own turn: Christ, the *firstfruits*; then, when he comes, those who belong to him. (1 Cor 15:20-23)

In Paul's mind, it is as if Adam and Christ are two firstfruits: one the firstfruit of death, the other the firstfruit of life. In fact, the idea of firstfruits runs like a backbone under the flesh of 1 Corinthians 15.

In verse 4 he wrote that Christ "was raised *on the third day* according to the Scriptures." Which Scriptures was he thinking of? Before anything else, almost certainly Genesis 1 and the third day of creation. There we read (and note how the repetition drives home the point): "Then God said, 'Let the land produce vegetation: *seed-bearing plants and trees on the land that bear fruit with seed in it, according to their various kinds.*' And it was so. The land produced vegetation: *plants bearing seed according to their kinds* and trees bearing *fruit with seed in it according to their kinds*" (Gen 1:11-12).

There on the third day of Genesis 1 we see the first fruits of creation (as Christ, raised on the third day, would be the first fruit of the *new* creation, of resurrection from the dead). These "firstfruits" each reproduce "according to their kinds" because they have seed— the next generation—*within* them. Thus *what happens to the fruit happens to the seed.* So it is, says Paul, with Adam and Christ. They are the firstfruits of two very different crops: one of death, the other of life. All others are but seed in one of those fruits.

Have you ever noticed that when Paul writes of Adam and Christ, he writes as if they were the only men in the world, as if no others existed? That was the big picture of humanity for Paul. It is not that humanity is a vast throng of disconnected individuals. Adam and Christ are *the* two men: the heads, the firstfruits of the old and the new human race. Each one of us is merely a seed in one of those fruits, a member of one of their bodies, dependent for our fate, not on ourselves but on the fruit in which we belong. When Adam sinned, we sinned in him; when he died, we died. At my birth I was born into a sinful, guilty, dead humanity. I was born into *that* identity (an identity I then managed to live out rather well).

While we're here, we simply must have a quick taste of that spicy little verse, Hebrews 7:10. Here's the context: Hebrews has been telling the story of how, back in Genesis 14, Abraham gave a "tithe" or tenth of what he had to the great king Melchizedek. And here's the fun bit: according to Hebrews, Abraham's great-grandson

Levi (who wasn't born yet in Genesis 14), could *also* be said to have paid that tithe "through Abraham, because when Melchizedek met Abraham, Levi was still in the body of his ancestor" (verses 9-10). Yet to be born, Levi was considered to be still "in Abraham." He was, after all, Abraham's descendant, his "seed." He was still in the old fruit. And so what Abraham did, he did. It's all very much what was going on with Adam, the father of humanity. To use the language of Hebrews: we sinned, we were declared guilty, and we died through Adam *because* when Adam sinned we were still in the body of our ancestor.

Today most of us live in a world of hyperindividualism, and so such talk of our union with Adam or union with Christ sounds weird—and as factual as a unicorn. Because we think we don't *really* have any unity with Adam, it even sounds unfair. Why must *I* suffer because of what *he* did? (As if *really* each of us *were* islands, independent of him.) But that individualism has mutilated our

One fun old legend has it that the place of Jesus' crucifixion, Golgotha (from the Aramaic for "skull"), was so named for being the site of Adam's tomb. Thus artistic depictions of the cross often show Jesus' blood dripping down from the cross onto Adam's skull, the Last Adam bringing life to the First.

view of the Christian good news, turning it into a *little* message, an ad for the consumer: "Come and add something to your life . . . have some grace." Paul saw it very differently. He saw a far deeper problem and a far grander vision. Our plight, he saw, is not merely that we each fail to be good enough and need a little forgiveness. If it were that simple, of course we'd be tempted to try a bit harder and turn up the morality. Instead, our very *identity* is a problem. We were born of Adam. There is no hope for us in trying harder or getting some divine leniency. Our only hope is to be taken out of Adam's old humanity, to be born *again* into a new humanity, to be a new creation.

How, then, on that dark day of the fall, must Adam and Eve have thrilled to hear of the Seed, the offspring, the child who would bruise the serpent's head (Gen 3:15)! Nothing else would suffice. Born not of a man but the seed of *woman*, a son who must then be provided specially by God. Here was the hope of life for Adam and all in him. And so affected was Adam with this news that he gives the woman a new name (Gen 3:20). When a person is given a new name in Scripture—whether it be Abram-Abraham, Hoshea-Joshua, Saul-Paul or Simon-Peter—it is always of signal importance. So it is here. Previously, when he first set eyes on his wife, Adam called her "Woman" (Gen 2:23). But in light of the hope he now has he gives her a new name: "Eve" ("Life!"). Life would come to Adam's shrunken, dying race through a child. As John Henry Newman put it in his masterful hymn "Praise to the Holiest in the Height":

O loving wisdom of our God!
When all was sin and shame,
A second Adam to the fight
And to the rescue came.

Oh wisest love! that flesh and blood,
Which did in Adam fail,
Should strive afresh against the foe,
Should strive and should prevail.

The Lord Will Create a New Thing on Earth

And now we come to it: if the Son of God was to be the Last Adam, to undo the fall, to be the head of a new humanity, to be one with his people, his bride, then he needed to become human. He needed to be—in real, pinchable reality—what had so long been promised: the seed of woman. The Word become flesh.

THE LION OF LYONS

Irenaeus, the second-century bishop of Lyons in Gaul, was one of those men with a serious claim to fame: his childhood mentor had been the great Polycarp, a martyr who as a youngster had known the apostle John. A direct link to the apostles, with the stories to prove it! But that was nothing next to his ability as a theologian.

Irenaeus believed that Christ was all about undoing what Adam had done. More than saving a few souls, Christ would make Adam's disaster—the catastrophe that makes all creation groan in pain—start working *backwards*. Irenaeus argued that Genesis 3 followed straight on from Genesis 2 without any break in time, meaning that the fall happened on the sixth day of creation. Thus Adam and Eve never got to enjoy God's rest on the seventh day, the Saturday. Bad Friday. But this was just what Christ came to reverse: as sin and death came into the world through a tree on Bad Friday, so sin and death would be defeated on a tree on Good Friday. Adam fell by heeding Satan's temptation to eat; Christ conquered by resisting just that temptation in the wilderness.

This is perhaps why, in his Gospel, John (who always loved hinting at hidden theological meaning) records two rather strange moments in Jesus' ministry, one at the very beginning, one at the very end. Twice we hear Jesus speak to Mary his mother and call her "Woman": at the wedding at Cana (Jn 2:4) and on the cross (Jn 19:26). It's hardly the way you expect the perfect son to address his mother. It doesn't exactly exude loving warmth. (The translators of the 1984 New International Version, feeling awkward about it, added some cushioning, making Jesus say, "*Dear* woman," in each case. Problem solved.) But perhaps it was another deliberate attempt to make it clear that, in first showing his glory at Cana and in finally dying on the cross, he was the promised seed of *woman*. For on the

In a garden, Adam fell down into death; in a garden tomb, Christ rose up from it.

So Christ would restore the creation that sin had ravaged; he would gently rehumanize us, bringing us back to what we were made to be. But more: the Son of Man would have a glory that the first man had never known. His new creation would surpass the old creation. With this glorious one, we would gain far more than we ever lost in Adam. "For if, by the trespass of the one man, death reigned through that one man, *how much more* will those who receive God's abundant provision of grace and of the gift of righteousness reign in life through the one man, Jesus Christ" (Rom 5:17).

Irenaeus (c. 130–c. 202)

cross he was the long-expected offspring of the woman, finally crushing the serpent's head.

Yet while he needed to become human, there was a fairly obvious problem in so doing. If Adam's sin really did lead to condemnation for all humanity, how could he become human and not himself be condemned like everyone else? How could he save his people from their sin if he too was born with the very sin that ran in the veins of Adam's race? Ever since Genesis 4, men have fathered children in their own sinful image and likeness. Flesh has given birth to flesh (Jn 3:6). What was needed was a new thing: Christ must be born of woman, but he must have no human father in whose image and likeness he would otherwise be. Like Adam, he must have no father but God. A virgin would need to conceive him by the pure power of the Holy Spirit (Is 7:14; Lk 1:35) and would thus give birth to a spiritual, holy one (Jn 3:6). And so, just as the Spirit hovered over the waters in Genesis, he would overshadow Mary, that the one to be born might be the head of a *new* humanity and a *new* creation.

As well as avoiding the inherited sin of Adam, through the virgin birth Christ showed that his salvation and his new human race are *miraculous*. Joseph and Mary, however much they might have wanted it, could never have produced the Savior of the world by themselves. Jesus' blessed and beautiful life is not an instance of some superhumanity we can aspire to by our own efforts. He is not the product of an evolutionary leap, the unfolding of our race's inner potential. *We* have not joined God and humankind together. Mary simply received the word of God as a gift from heaven: *that* is how we can have Christ's new life. The virgin birth is an almighty No! to all our silly attempts at earning salvation.

It means that before Jesus is ever an example to us, a model of love and goodness, he is something we *cannot* be. In his birth of a virgin he was not giving us an example; he was coming as a Savior. The volcanic Reformer Martin Luther believed it critical for our health that we get this clear: "The chief article and foundation of the gospel," he wrote, "is that *before you take Christ as an example, you accept and recognize him as a gift*, as a present that God has given you and that is your own."[3] Otherwise, Christ is of little more help to us than any other good man. And then we have no good news at all. Small wonder, then, that

The Annunciation by Fra Angelico, c. 1431. Gabriel announces the virgin birth of Christ as the Holy Spirit comes upon Mary.

whenever the virgin birth has been demythologized or denied by theologians, the invariable consequence has been a loss of the gospel in their theology. The virgin birth of Jesus guards the very goodness of the Christian good news: here is a supernatural intervention and salvation.

Jesus Is Our Brother Now

My mind goes quite giddy and I get goose bumps as I write this: *God has come to be with us!* The Lord of glory has made himself a closer friend than any other. No, not just close: the Bridegroom has made himself *one* with his dear bride. Because of what the Son of God has done, I can now say that I am flesh of his flesh and bone of his bone. All he *is* he has given to us, so that all he *has* he can share with us.

In the early days after the New Testament, there were some who just could not believe that God himself could have become truly human. One understands: it does seem almost incredible. But rather than marvel, they dismissed the very possibility and said that Christ must only have *seemed* to be human (they were thus known as "docetists," from the Greek word *dokein*, meaning "to seem"). Christ, they argued, was a spirit. Therefore he didn't really eat, breathe or die; he didn't even really leave footprints, they said. Rather, he only *pretended* to eat in front of his shortsighted disciples; he *pretended* to walk, while all along floating through the world like a holy smell.

Straight to the point, the apostle John uncompromisingly condemned such thinking, writing that "Many deceivers, *who do not acknowledge Jesus Christ as coming in the flesh*, have gone out into the world. Any such person is the deceiver and the antichrist" (2 Jn 7). Following his lead, many of the church's heavyweights stepped into the ring to confront this weirdness, and over the centuries they pinned the reluctant down to a concession: maybe Jesus *was* human . . . but at least, he can't have had a human mind. Enter Gregory of Nazianzus (theologian, tenth degree black belt). Gregory had fueled himself up on Hebrews 2:14 (*"Since the children have*

flesh and blood, [Christ] shared in their humanity so that by his death
he might destroy him who holds the power of death"). With that
he got the stranglehold on his opponents, writing, "What [Christ]
has not assumed he has not healed."[4] That is, Christ took or assumed our flesh and blood *in order to heal it* of its sin: he would
take it through death into a new life and bring it back to God. But
if there is any part of our humanity that he did *not* take, then that
will not be healed by him. What Gregory had seen with limpid
clarity was that *Jesus'* humanity is essential for the salvation of *our*
humanity. He simply could not be the head of a new humanity if he
was not truly human. He could not be our kinsman-redeemer or
the true Bridegroom of his people if we were not flesh of his flesh.

Today, all this seems rather foreign and exotic, does it not? "Jesus
saves from sin" we know well. "Jesus heals flesh" has the feel of
something from outside our comfortable shire. But by coming in a
body, Christ came to give a hope and a future *to our bodies.* After all,
Christ came not to replace but to redeem the very creation he had
designed and declared good: bodies, trees, lions, lambs, all of it. To
do that, though, and to share his life with the humanity he had
created, *he had to take it to himself.* Life is found only *in him*, after all
(Jn 1:4). To heal this race of Adam, he could not just appear in a body,
cobbled together and brought down from heaven; he had to take
Adam's flesh and blood. Of course, he could have started a *wholly* new
human race by taking dust afresh from the ground, as he'd done with
Adam. But that would do us no good. The old race of Adam would
be left entirely unaffected by what he did. Outlandish it may sound,
but we must say it: no umbilical cord of connection, no redemption!

God Himself Is Born

So Christ was truly human. But we must also say that he was truly
God. He could only ever share with us what he himself had, so if
he is not God, how could he share with us the life of God? If he is
not truly the beloved Son of God, how could he ever make us the

sons of God? If he never had the confidence to cry "Abba" to the Almighty, how could he give us any boldness before the throne? Our salvation is only as good as it is *because* Christ is who he is. Make him less than God and you make the gospel less than good: no free access to know a fatherly God as his beloved children.

Perhaps even more than Jesus' true humanity, his deity has been a hard one for many to swallow. Some simply deny it, calling him a good man or a great angel. But you cannot call yourself a *Christian* and hold such views, not after John wrote this: "Who is the liar? It is whoever denies that Jesus is the Christ. Such a person is the antichrist—denying the Father and the Son. No one who denies the Son has the Father; whoever acknowledges the Son has the Father also" (1 Jn 2:22-23).

However, there have also been Christians who have been *shy* of affirming that Jesus is the Lord, the eternal Son of God. Take Theodore of Mopsuestia, a fourth-century bishop whose confusion was due, perhaps, to being saddled with such a name. According to him, "Jesus is similar to all other men, *differing from natural men in nothing except that [the Word] has given him grace.*"[5] In other words, Jesus is not the Son of God: the Son or Word of God has *a relationship with the man Jesus*, helping him along, giving him grace. Be strong, reader! And before you laugh or vomit, see how this view of Jesus changes the shape of the gospel. Here, salvation is about us being given a bit of a boost by some abstract blessing called "grace." What it meant was that, for Theodore, Jesus became more of a model than a savior: a man *helped along* by God. And if God helps us in the same way that he helped Jesus, then we too can be just as holy and righteous as him. I wrote that this "changes the shape of the gospel"; perhaps it would be more accurate to say it *undoes* the gospel. For this is salvation by assisted works. And another problem: if God is not actually prepared to become one of us and die for us, he clearly can't love us that much. He certainly doesn't love as much as the God who will. Even if he is prepared to throw us the odd bun, such a God must prefer to keep himself to himself.

Shortly after Theodore died, a council of church leaders met in Ephesus to discuss this sort of take on Jesus. They weren't impressed. No, so right is it to say that Jesus is the Son of God that Mary, they declared, can be called the "God-bearer." She bore God the Son himself in her womb as he took on flesh. It meant they were left with a very different gospel. For them, it was not so much that Christ is a model; first and foremost he is the Savior of the helpless. And his salvation is not about God, from a distance, lobbing down some sort of help, some "grace"; here, God graciously gives us *himself* and his own life. *God* is the blessing of the gospel. God with us.

The Rising Sun Will Come to Us from Heaven

In the life of Jesus, then, we see two marvelous things: we see *the Son of God* revealing his Father's compassionate heart and purposes; and we see *the Son of Man* living in sweet fellowship with God. No wonder "many prophets and righteous people longed to see" this great sight (Mt 13:17)!

"He stilled the storm to a whisper; the waves of the sea were hushed" (Ps 107:29). *The Storm on the Sea of Galilee* by Rembrandt, 1633.

First, *the Son of God.* That Jesus is the Son of God is central to how the Gospels portray him. John makes it clear that this is precisely why he wrote his Gospel: "that you may believe that Jesus is the Messiah, the Son of God, and that by believing you may have life in his name" (Jn 20:31). Matthew, Mark and Luke show the key events in Jesus' life being all about his identity as the Son of God. As a child he gravitates to the temple as his "Father's house" (Lk 2:49); at his baptism and transfiguration, God declares him to be his beloved Son (Lk 3:21-22; 9:28-36); in the wilderness, the phrase repeated on the tempter's lips is "*If* you are the Son of God . . ." (Mt 4:6); a pivot point is Peter's confession "You are the Messiah, the Son of the living God" (Mt 16:16); at his trial he is asked if he is the Son of God (Mk 14:61-62); and at his death the centurion recognizes that he is (Mk 15:39). And we could go on.

In the eternal Son of God, the exact imprint of his Father's being, we see just what God is truly—and so surprisingly—like. He is, after all, God himself come to tabernacle with us. He is the temple, the dwelling place of God, the place filled with the glory of God (Jn 2:21). In him, divine light shines once again in the darkness.

And what do we find? Not purposeless self-announcement; in the coming of the Son of God we see the ushering in of a kingdom—the kingdom of God—which fulfills every human dream. The coming of the kingdom of God means the driving out of the evil that oppresses us. "If it is by the Spirit of God that I drive out demons," said Jesus, "then the kingdom of God has come upon you" (Mt 12:28). It is like a treasure, a great pearl, a wedding feast, and yet it is for the poor in spirit (Mt 5:3). It means the healing of the sick, the raising of the dead, the cleansing of lepers, the casting out of demons (Mt 10:7). It is a kingdom of the humble (Mt 18:4). It means judgment on evil and self-righteousness, the provision of daily bread, and welcome for the outcasts. It is the binding up of the broken, the forgiveness of sin, the beginning of the renewal of all things. That is why the heart cry of the Christian is "your kingdom come"—for what a kingdom! What a God who would so reign!

John the Baptist's father, Zechariah, prophesied of his son:

You will go on before the Lord to prepare the way for him,
    to give his people the knowledge of salvation
through the forgiveness of their sins,
    because of the tender mercy of our God,

by which the rising sun will come to us from heaven
    to shine on those living in darkness
and in the shadow of death,
    to guide our feet into the path of peace. (Lk 1:76-79)

That is just what we see in Jesus: as he is filled with compassion for the crowds, harassed and helpless; as he groans with pity for the leper; as he weeps over Jerusalem; we see the tender mercy of God himself.

The Perfect Human

Now here's the wonder of the Son of Man: the loving relationship that the Son has always enjoyed with his Father *he now brings to us*. When he becomes a man, for the first time *a human being* enjoys the Son's own fellowship with and standing before the Father. In Jesus, for the first time there is *a human being* living in perfect fellowship with God. Loving God with all his heart, soul, mind and strength, loving his neighbor as himself, he is the first ever to keep and fulfill the law of God. You see the contrast to all others in his temptation in the wilderness: where Adam had listened to the tempter and eaten; where Israel failed in the desert, Christ remains utterly loyal to God. Nobody had heard of such a thing before: a faithful human! Though *faithful*

hardly captures it: he loves his Father so completely that it is as food to him to do his Father's will (Jn 4:34); zeal for his Father's house consumes him (Jn 2:16-17). This is what he brings to share with humanity: his own sonship, his own relationship and life with his Father.

Marriage at Cana, **from Niels Hemmingsen's** *Postil*, **1576**

And what a life! Christians often use a negative, chilly word to describe Christ's life: it was *sinless*. That tells us what he was *not*: he was *not* selfish, cruel, abusive, twisted, petty or proud. Now, when opened out like that, we can see that to be "sinless" is beautiful, dynamic and attractive. The trouble is, we often leave the word closed, and then it reinforces all our stereotypes of what "holy people" are like: bloodless, bland, dreamy, delicate and so spiritual it looks painful.

But what *was* he like? Anything but boring and anemic! Here was a man with towering charisma, running over with life. Health and healing, loaves and fishes, all abounded in his presence. So compelling did people find him that crowds thronged round him. Men, women, children, sick and mad, rich and poor: they found him so magnetic some wanted just to touch his clothes. Kinder than summer, he befriended the rejects and gave hope to the hopeless. The dirty and despised found they *mattered* to him. His closest friends found that, as the Son of Man came eating and drinking, being with him was like being with a bridegroom at a wedding. Robert Law wrote:

> The blessings of the Divine Kingdom He was bringing to men He could compare to nothing so much as to the festive joys of marriage (St. Mark ii.19). Himself and His disciples were like a wedding-party. He was the bridegroom whose joy overflows into the hearts of his friends, and turns fasting into feasting. Even at the last, on the verge of Gethsemane and in sight of Calvary, He speaks not of His sorrows, but still of His joy. He is the Lord of joy, and His crowning desire for His servants is that they may enter into the joy of their Lord and have it fulfilled in them. Yet Jesus is the Man of Sorrows; and it is because He is the Man of Sorrows that His joy is so precious a legacy, so strong an anchor to our souls.[6]

Yes, he was a man who felt a world of pain, yet who abounded with joy.

Generous and genial, firm and resolute, he was always surprising. Loving but not soppy, his insight unsettled people and his kindness won them. Indeed, he was a man of extraordinary—and extraordinarily appealing—contrasts. You simply couldn't make him up, for you'd make him only one or the other. He was red-blooded and human, but not rough. Pure, but never dull. Serious with sunbeams of wit. Sharper than cut glass, he out-argued all comers, but never for the sake of the win. He knew no failings in himself, yet was transparently humble. He made the grandest claims for himself, yet without a whiff of pomposity. He ransacked the temple, spoke of hellfire, called Herod a fox, the Pharisees pimped-up corpses, and yet never do you doubt his love as you read his life.

THE LIFE OF GOD IN HUMANITY

What we see so gorgeously displayed in Jesus is *the life of God in humanity*, fleshed out for us to see. *That* is what the life of God is like. The eternal Son of God has always been characterized by such love, such purity and vivaciousness, but now he has brought his life *to us*, to be the firstborn of the new humanity, and this is how humanity complete in him looks. Here in the Son of Man is both the *identity* and the *character* of the new humanity.

Those who are found in Christ find themselves *beloved* like him (that is their new status): as the Father looks with pleasure and delight on this perfect Son of his, so he looks with pleasure and delight on all who are in him. Just as we were born into the sinful status of Adam, believers are born again into the righteous, beloved status of the Son. He lived *for* us, and his righteous life is ours.

And those who are found in Christ begin to find themselves *loving* like him (that is their new character). Of this new humanity of his, sharing his nature, we begin to love God and other people, and hate evil, as Christ does. We begin to be, like him, ever more *alive*.

With a huge heart, he hated evil and felt for the needy. He loved God and he loved people. You look at him and you have to say, "Here is a man truly alive, unwithered in any way, far more vital and vigorous, far more full and complete, far more *human* than any other."

The Anointed One

The question is, how? Where does this life of God in the new humanity come from? And the answer is given by Gabriel, when he announced to Mary the birth of Christ: "*The Holy Spirit* will come on you, and the power of the Most High will overshadow you. So the holy one to be born will be called the Son of God" (Lk 1:35). The Son or Word of God has never acted alone but always in the power of the Spirit (as for example in Genesis 1, when the Word of God is spoken into the darkness borne by the Spirit). So inseparable are they that Psalm 33:6 can sing, "By *the word of the* LORD were the heavens made, their starry host by *the breath* [or *Spirit*] of his mouth." And as it had always been, so it was when the Word became flesh: he did all that he did in the power of the Spirit.

Born in the power of the Spirit, he lives and acts as a man in the power of the Spirit. At his baptism in the Jordan, the Spirit anoints him, then sends him into the lifeless wilderness just as he had once sent him into the lifeless void in Genesis 1. Returning to Galilee in the power of the Spirit, he announced and defined his ministry in the synagogue at Nazareth using the words of Isaiah 61:

> *The Spirit of the Lord is on me*,
>> because he has anointed me
>> to proclaim good news to the poor.
> He has sent me to proclaim freedom for the prisoners
>> and recovery of sight for the blind,
> to set the oppressed free,
>> to proclaim the year of the Lord's favor." (Lk 4:18-19)

So he healed, did good, and drove out demons—all in the power of the Spirit (Mt 12:28; Acts 10:38). Later he would offer himself up on the cross by the Spirit (Heb 9:14) and be raised from the dead by the power of the Spirit (Rom 8:11).

In the Old Testament, kings, priests and even prophets would be consecrated to their ministries through being anointed with poured oil (sometimes called the "oil of joy," as in Psalm 45:7), symbolic of the outpoured Spirit. As the true king of Israel, David's son, the king of kings (Jn 1:49); as the great high priest (Heb 4:14) and the long-expected ultimate prophet (Deut 18:15), Jesus was anointed with the Spirit. For he is *the* Anointed One ("the Christ" in Greek, "the Messiah" in Hebrew); he is the fruitful tree of life fed by the streams of living water (Ps 1).

Christ shows what it is to be a human, fully alive in the Spirit. And he is the head of a new, Spirit-filled humanity: all in him share in this anointing of his. All his new humanity are, like him, "children born not of natural descent, nor of human decision or a husband's will, but born of God" by the power of the Spirit (Jn 1:13). Then, reborn in Christ, we drink of the same living waters, and we begin to flow with his exuberant love and life:

> So it is written: "The first man Adam became a living being"; the last Adam, a life-giving spirit. The spiritual did not come first, but the natural, and after that the spiritual. The first man was of the dust of the earth, the second man is of heaven. As was the earthly man, so are those who are of the earth; and as is the heavenly man, so also are those who are of heaven. And just as we have born the image of the earthly man, so shall we bear the image of the heavenly man. (1 Cor 15:45-49)

3

There and Back Again

The King in His Beauty

"All that I am I give to you, and all that I have I share with you," says the bride to her groom on their wedding day. This is a profound mystery, but I am talking about the cross. For on the cross we shared with Christ *all* that we have. Born of Mary, he had already come to share our flesh and blood; on the cross we then gave to him all our sin, our death, our shame. The loving Bridegroom took the sorrows and sickness of his Bride down to death to bury them forever.

The ballad of the wedding day can be heard in Psalm 45, where the king, enthralled with his royal bride, brings her into his palace. It is a psalm that may well have been used at (one of the many!) royal weddings in Israel, but the king it actually depicts is quite unique. Of him it is said: "Your throne, *O God*, will last for ever" (Ps 45:6). The Bridegroom-King *is* God, the anointed Son (Heb 1:8-9). And he is described, literally, as being "the most *handsome* of men" (Ps 45:2 NRSV). Naturally. Jesus the Son was eternally the spotless epitome of beauty.

Yet for his Bride this beautiful one would be lifted up on the cross and there disfigured.

See, my servant will act wisely;
  he will be raised and *lifted up* and highly exalted.
Just as there were many who were appalled at him—

his appearance was so disfigured beyond that of any human
  being
and his form marred beyond human likeness. (Is 52:13-14)

His beard pulled out, his body pierced and lacerated, bloodied,
beaten and spat upon: the king in his beauty became gruesome and
horrifying to behold. But that was just the point. As Isaiah went on:

> Surely he took up *our* pain
>   and bore *our* suffering,
> yet we considered him punished by God,
>   stricken by him, and afflicted.
> But he was pierced for *our* transgressions,
>   he was crushed for *our* iniquities;
> the punishment that brought *us* peace was on *him*,
>   and by *his* wounds *we* are healed. (Is 53:4-5)

Out of sheer and boundless love for his Bride, he took her sicknesses
upon himself, with all the consequences of her sin. He took her

ugliness that she might have
his loveliness.

And yet. It is in that very
moment, when he is made
most physically appalling, that
he becomes most dear to us.
"Christ was never more lovely
to his church than when he
was most deformed for his
church," wrote Richard Sibbes.[1]
For in his willingness to die
our death and take our sufferings upon himself, he reveals the utter vigor and ardor
of his love. And we are not the

The Crucifixion **by Lucas Cranach the Elder, 1502**   only ones stirred. For eternity, the Father had an unsurpassable pleasure in his Son, but that delight overflowed when Jesus proved his character at the cross. "The reason my Father loves me is that I lay down my life," said Jesus (Jn 10:17). Like ours, the heart of the Father in heaven is inflamed with delight at his Son's faithfulness and compassion.

It all means that the cross is a place thick with irony and paradox: there the beautiful one is vile, the holy one is placed between criminals, the high and mighty one is lifted up, *but to die.* For on that day, so altogether different from his eternal life, Jesus proved most definitively who he is and what he is like. The centurion exclaimed, "Surely this man was the Son of God" (Mk 15:39); the soldiers crowned him with thorns, wrapped him in imperial purple and "worshiped" him; Pilate put above his head the notice "JESUS OF NAZARETH, THE KING OF THE JEWS" (Jn 19:19). They all spoke and acted better than they knew, or in mockery—for it was all true. There was the Son of God being so *himself* that even a Gentile executioner sensed it. On the cross we see the Bridegroom, loving to death; the Lord of glory, giving out his life; the Lord of hosts, crushing Satan; the King, enthroned. We see *Jesus* ("the Lord saves"). This is who he is. As the Orthodox sing on Good Friday:

He who clothes himself with light as with a garment
Stood naked at the judgement.
On his cheek he received blows
From the hands which he had formed.
The lawless multitude nailed to the Cross
The Lord of glory.

Today is hanged upon the tree
He who hanged the earth in the midst of the waters.
A crown of thorns crowns him
Who is the king of the angels.
He is wrapped about with the purple of mockery
Who wraps the heaven in clouds.[2]

It is all too easy to shear the cross of its glory by treating it as a cold transaction *apart from Christ*. But the crucified one *is* the glory of the cross. There in almighty kindness he takes our sin and defeats our death *that we might have him*. And when *he* is lifted up in the message of the cross, he will draw all people to himself (Jn 12:32).

THE CROSS ALONE IS OUR THEOLOGY

"The cross alone is our theology." So said the Reformer Martin Luther. After all, if the one nailed to the cross truly is Immanuel—God with us—then we desperately need to rethink what God is like. What kind of God is this who would bleed and die for us? This is not the kind of Supreme Being I naturally imagine when my mind goes gallivanting. Settled cozily in my armchair, I tend to assume that God must be rather like me. Bigger and better, I concede, but basically like me. Me on cosmic steroids. Then I see the cross, and it is like a defibrillator for the mind.

There on the cross is displayed the glory, the wisdom, the righteousness, the love, the justice, and the power of God (1 Cor 1:18-31). And none of it looks anything like what you'd expect. Would you ever have thought a man dying on a cross was the definition of love? Yet this is how we know what love is (1 Jn 3:16). Would you ever have looked at the miscarriage of justice that was his trial and imagined that there, above all, is displayed the perfect justice of God? Yet God did it to demonstrate his justice (Rom 3:26). Would you ever have dreamed that the Almighty would make the definitive display of his power there, nailed to a cross between common criminals? There *seems* to be *nothing* powerful about that man in the throes of death. Yet, hanging there, he is crushing the head of the Serpent, tying up the strong man, driving out the prince of this world, destroying death, putting the spiritual powers to open shame and triumphing over them. On the cross we see true, pure power, used as it should be: to bless. "And so," wrote T. F.

Torrance, "the cross with all its incredible meekness and patience and compassion is no deed of passive and beautiful heroism simply, but the most potent and aggressive deed that heaven and earth have ever known: the attack of God's holy love upon the inhumanity of man and the tyranny of evil, upon all the piled up contradiction of sin."[3]

Adam sought knowledge from the tree, and died; Christ died on his tree and won for us a knowledge altogether more wonderful: the knowledge of God. In other words, on the cross we are given not only the sweet *salvation* of God but the counterintuitive *revelation* of God. On the cross we see how humble, how self-giving, how perfectly generous and compassionate the living God is. That is why Luther wanted all thinking about God to be done in the shadow of the cross.

And all thinking about ourselves, in fact. For as the cross reveals God to us, so in the same moment it unmasks us. His light shows up our darkness. It happened first to the crowds in Jerusalem: their bloodthirsty fickleness and guilt were bared by his quiet innocence. And we fare no better. The humility of the Son of God, descending from glory to Golgotha, exposes our pride in all its foolishness, pettiness and ugliness. His use of power exposes our horrid abuse of it. His rampant kindness exposes our slovenly selfishness. His very graciousness judges us. His coming to save proves our need and our plight. In the cross we see not only God's goodness; we see our own perversion.

Crucified with Christ

So Christ died in our place and suffered where we did not. But he was the Last Adam, the head of the new humanity, and therefore, just as all who are born in Adam share Adam's fate, so all who are reborn in Christ share his. All who are members of Christ's body experience what happened to that body. *We died with him.* Our old identity was slaughtered, speared and buried with Christ (Col 2:12; Rom 6:3). His death, not our sin, is our past.

Christ in the Sepulchre, Guarded by Angels by
William Blake, c. 1805

It means the most welcome relief and freedom from our society's terrible insistence on the virtue of self-confidence. I know, self-confidence sounds so right and wonderful. It's like caffeine for the ego—for however long you manage to keep it up. The thing is, though, if you try to have self-confidence before God and in yourself you'll be a sorry emotional yo-yo. Up on Sunday because you've been to church and prayed, down on Monday because you haven't. All because you assume you yo-yo in and out of God's favor based on how *you* do or feel. "God loves me; he loves me not." (I've done well = he loves me; I've failed = he loves me not.) That's how it must be when *you* are the grounds of your confidence.

Reliance on ourselves is no option in light of the cross. However fantastically marvelous we may think we are, the cross is God's verdict on us as sinners. It annihilates even the possibility of finally placing our trust in ourselves. Meaning we can know a far greater assurance, anchoring it in firm ground outside ourselves, in Christ. Christians are people who have given up all claims to both our badness *and* our goodness—and instead gotten *him*. Thus it is with no self-confidence but all boldness that Paul can write, "I have been crucified with Christ and I no longer live, but Christ lives in me" (Gal 2:20). Or again, "May I never boast except in the cross of our Lord Jesus Christ, through which the world has been crucified to me, and I to the world. Neither circumcision nor uncircumcision means anything; what counts is the new creation" (Gal 6:14-15). Since he was *in* Christ, he knew he had been taken down into the death of Christ. There, all boasting in himself was silenced. He had been condemned. More than that, in fact: there in the death of Christ he had met and endured *all* his condemnation.

Martin Luther once wrote to a young friend of his who was struggling with guilt and failure:

> When the devil throws our sins up to us and declares that we deserve death and hell, we ought to speak thus: "I admit that I deserve death and hell. What of it? Does this mean that I shall be sentenced to eternal damnation? By no means. For I know One who suffered and made satisfaction in my behalf. His name is Jesus Christ, the Son of God. Where he is, there I shall be also."[4]

It's just the answer for the Christian dogged by failure and the whisperings of the accuser. Instead of trying to top up the work of the cross by offensive attempts to buy God off, and instead of trying to sweep our guilt under improved behavior, we can own up to it, knowing it can no longer define us. We have a new identity in Christ: we died with him; and now where he is in newness of life, there we shall be also.

At the cross, Pilgrim's burden rolled away

The Firstborn from Among the Dead

At Jesus' baptism, the heavens had opened and the Father had declared his sheer pleasure in his Son. And now, after the cross, when the Son had so perfectly displayed the extent of his love, the Father could not leave his beloved one dead. So he vindicated—or "*justified*"—him, declaring him utterly worthy of life (1 Tim 3:16), declaring him with power through the Spirit to be the Son of God (Rom 1:4).

That greatest declaration brought about the greatest event since the creation of the world: the inauguration of the new creation. Bursting through death, out of the grave, the Son overturned the old order—or disorder, we should say—of Adam. The reign of death and corruption was undone, and a human being now stood, body and soul, wholly beyond the reach of the curse. J. R. R. Tolkien called that moment a *eucatastrophe*, "the greatest 'eucatastrophe' possible," in fact. That is, the resurrection was a catastrophic event, but a *good* catastrophic event. Or, to be more precise, a eucatastrophe is "the *sudden happy turn* in a story which pierces you with a joy that brings tears . . . your whole nature chained in material cause and effect, the chain of death, feels a sudden relief as if a major limb out of joint had suddenly snapped back."[5]

The Risen Lord by Lucas Cranach, 1558

Where the guilt of Adam had brought death, the righteousness of Christ brought victorious life. And clearly there was more righteousness in him than there was sin in us, for having borne our sin, death could no longer hold him. Having taken sin and death down to death, death had no further claim on him.

That otherwise unremarkable tomb in Jerusalem thus became the womb of a new creation. From it emerged the firstborn from the dead, the firstfruits of a royal harvest of life. The humanity, the flesh and bones that had been weak and corruptible in Adam were now triumphant and incorruptible. "On the third day," wrote G. K. Chesterton,

> the friends of Christ coming at day-break to the place found the grave empty and the stone rolled away. In varying ways they realised the new wonder; but even they hardly realised that the world had died in the night. What they were looking at was the first day of a new creation, with a new heaven and a new earth; and in a semblance of the gardener God walked again in the garden, in the cool not of the evening but the dawn.[6]

It was indeed a wondrous new beginning, like a new Eden, reestablishing all that God had once declared good: a human being—yes, God—walked in the garden, ruler over all things, in perfect harmony with God. Only now there would be no threat of death, no danger of a serpent to wreck it all. Death had been swallowed up in victory, the serpent crushed. The very creation would now wait in eager anticipation, longing to feel the full effects of his life as it had so long endured the fallout of Adam's curse. For the resurrection of the Firstborn was the guarantee that the creation itself would be liberated from its bondage to decay and brought into the glorious freedom of the Son of God (Col 1:18; Rom 8:21).

The Lord Our Righteousness

Think what the vindication of the head of the new humanity must mean. When Adam, the head of the old humanity, was found a sinner, all in him shared his fate. He was the firstfruit of death. When Christ was justified and declared worthy of life by his Father, he "was raised to life *for our justification*" (Rom 4:25). All in him share that life-giving justification he received on Easter morning. He is the third-day firstfruit of life and righteousness: all his seed that is *in him* share his fate. Thus in him *we* are given new life, and *we* become the very righteousness of God (2 Cor 5:21).

It all makes for an infinitely more nourishing and tasty gospel. Compare it to the McTheology where justification is explained as nothing more than God treating me "just as if I'd never sinned." I assumed this sort of thing as a young Christian. I believed—and was thrilled to believe—that when I first trusted in Christ, God had forgiven me all my sins. I had a clean slate. Lovely. The trouble was, I dirtied it up again rather fast. Now what was God to do with those new sins? Did I need to be *re*-justified? Well, certainly those sins were and are problems, hindering my *enjoyment* of the Christian life. But the notion that I might need to be rejustified betrayed the fact that I hadn't appreciated that my new identity as a Christian is *in Christ the righteous one*. Not my behavior, my feelings or my faithfulness: *he* is my righteousness (1 Cor 1:30). He is my status and my standing before God. The same yesterday, today and forever.

John Calvin used the story of Jacob from Genesis 27 to explain it:

> As [Jacob] did not of himself deserve the right of the first-born, concealed in his brother's clothing and wearing his brother's coat, which gave out an agreeable odor [Gen 27:27], he ingratiated himself with his father, so that to his own benefit he received the blessing while impersonating another. And we in like manner hide under the precious purity of our first-born brother, Christ, so that we may be attested righteous in God's sight. . . . And this is indeed the truth, for in order that we may appear before God's face unto salvation we must smell sweetly with his odor, and our vices must be covered and buried by his perfection.[7]

In other words, we are *clothed* with a righteousness that is not our own but Christ's. As Adam and Eve were clothed by the Lord in the skin of the first sacrificial animal (Gen 3:21), so Christians are clothed with Christ. Instead of having to face God in the fig leaves of our own efforts, we appear before the Father *in him*, "our vices covered and buried by his perfection." It isn't that Christians imagine silly spiritual shenanigans going on, Jesus wafting his righteousness to us through the ether while we sling him a package called "sin." We are clothed in his righteousness because we are *in him*, the Firstfruit. As Calvin put it: "We do not, therefore, contemplate [Christ] outside ourselves from afar in order that his righteousness may be imputed to us but because we put on Christ and are engrafted into his body—in short, because he deigns to make us one with him."[8]

How does anyone come to reign in life? Not through their own piety. Jesus said, "*Because I live*, you also will live" (Jn 14:19). My fate is determined by the head of the humanity or body to which I belong. To know my identity, you must look at my Head. If I belong to Adam, I share his guilt and his death is my destiny; if I belong to Christ, then it is his righteousness and his life which are mine. *All* Christians, then, no matter how weak, can boldly belt out Charles Wesley's fortifying words:

Isaac Blessing Jacob **by Gerrit Willemsz Horst, 1638**

No condemnation now I dread;
Jesus, and all in Him, is mine;
Alive in Him, my living Head,
And clothed in righteousness divine,
Bold I approach the eternal throne,
And claim the crown, through Christ my own.

My Beloved Is Mine, and I Am His

The risen Jesus is not only the firstborn and firstfruit of new life; like Adam, he is a bridegroom who shares his fate with his bride. Talking of Christ as a bridegroom became especially popular among the Reformers, who were looking for biblical images to illustrate salvation by grace alone. They didn't have to look hard, of course: Hosea and Song of Songs are whole books of the Bible dedicated to unpacking the truth that "your Maker is your husband" (Is 54:5); the story of the exodus is often looked back on by the prophets as the Lord's rescue of his bride (Ezek 16; Song 8:5); the people's faithlessness is routinely described as "adultery"; the end of all things is when "the wedding of the Lamb has come, and his bride has made herself ready" (Rev 19:7).

Martin Luther was the first of the Reformers to pick up the theme, telling the gospel as the story of a king (representing Jesus) marrying a poor girl of "ill repute" (representing us). At their wedding, she would say to him, "All that I am I give to you, and all that I have I share with you." In that moment, she shares with him all her debts and shame. Then the king would reply, "All that I am I give to you, and all that I have I share with you." At which, the wretched girl becomes the queen, and all the kingdom is hers. Just so, our great bridegroom has taken all our sin, our death, our judgment, and he shares with us all his life and perfect right-eousness. He has become poor that we might share his riches. It is the great marriage swap, or what Luther called the "joyful ex-change." Christ is one with his people, and so all theirs is his, and all his is theirs.[9]

The story tells the gospel so strikingly and so well that Refor-mation pastors and theologians loved to repeat it. The seventeenth-century London bookseller Edward Fisher gives a stirring example. Imagining a wise pastor speaking to a shaky, doubt-filled young Christian, he wrote:

The marriage union betwixt Christ and you is more than a bare
notion or apprehension of your mind; for it is a special, spiritual, and real union. . . . *Whence it must needs follow that you
cannot be condemned, except Christ be condemned with you;
neither can Christ be saved, except you be saved with him.* . . .
[For] when Christ hath married his spouse unto himself, he
passeth over all his estate unto her; so that whatsoever Christ
is or hath, you may boldly challenge as your own.[10]

Or, to take from a real-life wise pastor, here is how Fisher's contem-
porary, the sunny-hearted preacher Richard Sibbes said we can speak:

Often think with thyself, What am I? a poor sinful creature;
but I have a righteousness in Christ that answers all. I am
weak in myself, but Christ is strong, and I am strong in him.
I am foolish in myself, but I am wise in him. What I want [that
is, lack] in myself I have in him. He is mine, and his righteousness is mine, which is the righteousness of God-man.
Being clothed with this, I stand safe against conscience, hell,
wrath, and whatsoever. Though I have daily experience of my
sins, yet there is more righteousness in Christ, who is mine,
and who is the chief of ten thousand, than there is sin in me.[11]

And we can't stop there. The other gorgeous truth of the marriage between the risen Christ and his people is that the new life
we are given with him is no cold, contractual affair. We are not
brought to be mere acceptable serfs of a benevolent autocrat. No,
Christ *treasures* his bride. In Isaiah 62, God's people are told:

You will be a crown of splendour in the LORD's hand,
    a royal diadem in the hand of your God.
No longer will they call you Deserted,
    or name your land Desolate.
But you will be called Hephzibah ["my delight is in her"],
    and your land Beulah ["married"];

for the LORD will take delight in you . . .
as a bridegroom rejoices over his bride,
   so will your God rejoice over you. (Is 62:3-5)

His people are described as a crown: a precious treasure, a reward and
sign of honor. Just like a beloved wife, who is the crown of her
husband (Prov 12:4). And, astonishingly, she is not some odious
charity case for him: she makes his pupils dilate and his heart sing. He
delights in her and will not stop. She is truly, deeply, passionately *loved*.

Abba!

On Easter morning, Jesus was not only declared to be the Righteous
One, worthy of life; he was declared with power to be the *Son of God*.
Of course, he had always, eternally, been the Son of God. But this time
it was different. This time, when the Father said, "You are my Son;
today I have become your Father" (Heb 1:5), the Father was ad-
dressing *a man who had died*. Now a man—a man who had been

through death and all God's
judgment on evil—could be
known as the Son of God.
And once again, what is declared of him is true of all
who are *in* him: "You are all
sons of God through faith in
Christ Jesus, for all of you
who were baptized into
Christ have clothed your-
selves with Christ" (Gal
3:26-27 NIV 1984).

It is language to make
your eye screech to a halt
on the page: "You are all
sons"? In the midst of such

The Return of the Prodigal Son **by Pompeo Batoni, 1773**

ravishing truth, is this more of that first-century sexism we love to look down on with our contented chronological sneers? It is certainly no typo of Paul's: elsewhere he would write that all "who are led by the Spirit of God are *sons* of God" (Rom 8:14 NIV 1984). Not "children"; not "sons and daughters": *sons*. But it is not chauvinism that drives Paul's choice of words. He is seeking to be as clear as he can that the status *all* believers are given is, quite specifically, the status of the Son himself. Men who believe are part of the bride of Christ; women who believe are sons of God! For God does not give us some exalted but general standing before himself: the Son shares with us *his own sonship*.

This is precisely why Paul goes on in Romans 8, "the Spirit you received does not make you slaves, so that you live in fear again; rather, the Spirit you received brought about your adoption to sonship. And by him we cry, '*Abba*, Father'" (Rom 8:15). Or, as he puts it in Galatians 4:6: "Because you are his sons, God sent the Spirit of his Son into our hearts, the Spirit who calls out, '*Abba*, Father.'" Again, by inserting that Aramaic word *Abba* into his letters, Paul wakes you up to see that believers get to share the very cry of the Son himself. In the garden of Gethsemane, talking in private to his Father, Jesus had called him "*Abba*, Father" (Mk 14:36). Arguing that the Spirit of the Son makes *us* call out the very same words, Paul is demonstrating as intimately and visually as he can that in Christ we get to share the very relationship with the Father that the Son himself has always enjoyed. The personal name he has for his Father we are allowed to share. We can come before the Almighty and say—or stutter!—with a beloved son's own confidence, "Abba!"

Through the resurrection of Christ the firstborn, we who are in him are given life eternal. But we need to be specific about what that "life" is: it is life of the righteous and beloved Son. *That* is what we share. In the centuries after the New Testament, many liked to put it like this: the Son of God became human that we humans might become sons of God. Not mere forgiveness, and not some

abstract "heaven": *that* is the salvation he offers, because that is
who he is. It makes all the difference to *how* I live my new life. It
means I am not an employee under contract, afraid of being shown
the door the moment I fail; clothed in Christ (despite my many,
many failings) I can *always* cry "Abba!" It takes the sting out of the
accuser's hiss when I slip; it crucifies despair; it makes me want to
be with so loving a Father.

Is the Incarnation Over?

"It is a fundamental article of faith, that [Christ] is in the same body
in heaven wherein he conversed here on earth."[12] You can tell that
was written a long time ago (over three hundred years ago, in fact,
by John Owen). Nobody talks like that any more. And it's not just
the dusty turn of phrase; who today speaks of Christ's body in
heaven as a core part of Christianity? We hear umpteen sermons
on the cross and resurrection, but then it's as if he might as well
have evaporated, quietly disappearing into the ether. He died, he
rose, he vaporized. Which is less than comforting if he is our forerunner, blazing the trail for all who are in him.

But that is nothing like what we see in the New Testament. There
is no surreptitious discarding of his body, no floating off to realms
more cloudy: the one who says "Touch me and see; a ghost does
not have flesh and bones, as you see I have" (Lk 24:39) is the very
one who is "taken up into heaven" (Lk 24:51). He never abandons
humanity, even at the last minute; he never leaves the temple of his
body. Having taken on our humanity he faithfully bears it back to
heaven and back to his Father, like a good shepherd carrying home
his lost sheep.

When Adam sinned in Genesis 3, he was banished from the
Lord's presence in what is there called "the *Garden* of Eden": "So
the Lord God banished him from the Garden of Eden to work the
ground from which he had been taken. After he drove the man out,
he placed on the east side of the Garden of Eden cherubim and a

flaming sword flashing back and forth to guard the way to the tree of life" (Gen 3:23-24). But when Ezekiel speaks of what happened then, he describes "Eden, the garden of God" as "the holy *mount* of God" (Ezek 28:13-14). The sanctuary of Eden was a *mountain* garden, which explains how a river could flow out of it (Gen 2:10). Thus, when Adam was expelled from Eden, it was a *fall* from God's presence, down the mountain away from the company of the Lord.

Ever since then the cry has gone up: "LORD, who may dwell in your sacred tent? Who may live on your holy mountain?" (Ps 15:1). Who may go back up the mountain, past the cherubim, to eat from the tree of life and live with the Lord in peace forever? To which the understandable but crushing answer was given:

> The one whose walk is blameless
>> who does what is righteous,
>> who speaks the truth from their heart
> whose tongue utters no slander,
>> who does no wrong to a neighbor
>> and casts no slur on others,
> who despises a vile person
>> but honors those who fear the LORD,
> who keeps an oath even when it hurts,
>> and does not change their mind;
> who lends money to the poor without interest;
>> who does not accept a bribe against the innocent.
> *Whoever does these things*
>> *will never be shaken.* (Ps 15:2-5)

Which rules me out. Yet there is hope, for Psalm 16 goes straight on to tell of a righteous one who is everything just described. "I have set the LORD always before me," he says:

> Because he is at my right hand, *I shall not be shaken.*
> Therefore my heart is glad and my tongue rejoices;

my body also will rest secure,
because you will not abandon me to the grave,
   nor will you let your Holy One see decay.
You have made known to me the path of life;
   you will fill me with joy in your presence,
   with eternal pleasures at your right hand.
        (Ps 16:8-11 NIV 1984)

The Ascension of Christ by Dosso Dossi, 1520

In Jesus Christ we find the unshakably righteous Holy One who is worthy to live on God's holy hill. He is the Last Adam who ascends back up to be where the first Adam was: with God. Exodus 23:19 commands: "Bring the best of the firstfruits of your soil to the house of the LORD your God." *He* is the firstfruits and forerunner of the new humanity (the humanity that in Adam had first been taken from the soil or dust of the earth) now taken into the house of the Lord. It means that there is now a man, a real man with our flesh and blood, our experiences of the world, our humanity, in heaven. A man now sits next to God in perfect harmony. And a man with a "human hand will grasp us as we make our way into heaven. We shall be greeted by a face—the face of Jesus."[13]

THE HEART OF CHRIST IN HEAVEN
TOWARD SINNERS ON EARTH

Few have heard of Thomas Goodwin today, but there was a time when he was considered one of the theological greats, even hailed as "the greatest pulpit exegete of Paul that has ever lived."[14] Born in a small village in Norfolk, UK, in 1600, he grew up to be president of Magdalen College, Oxford, and one of the most beloved pastor-preachers of his day.

His most remarkable and most popular work was *The Heart of Christ in Heaven Toward Sinners on Earth*. His aim in it was clear and simple: Goodwin wanted to show through Scripture that for all Christ's heavenly majesty, seated on the throne, he is not now aloof from believers and unconcerned; he is still the same man, with the strongest affections for his people. In fact, if anything, his capacious heart beats *more* strongly than ever with tender love for them. Meaning we can approach the throne of grace with wonderful confidence, knowing we have a great high priest who can sympathize with our weaknesses, having been tempted in every way like us (Heb 4:14-16).

In particular, Goodwin argues, two things stir Christ's compassion: our afflictions and—almost unbelievably—our sins. Having experienced on earth the utmost load of pain, rejection and sorrow, Christ in heaven empathizes with our sufferings more fully than the most loving friend. More, though: he actually has compassion on his people who are "out of the way"—that is, sinning (Heb 5:2 KJV). Indeed, says Goodwin,

> your very sins move him to pity more than to anger . . . yea, his pity is increased the more toward you, even as the heart of a father is to a child that hath some loathsome disease . . . his hatred shall all fall, and that only upon the sin, to free you of it by its ruin and destruction, but his bowels shall be the more drawn out to you; and this as much when you lie under sin as under any other affliction. Therefore fear not, "What shall separate us from Christ's love?"[15]

His point is that those who are in Christ have a new identity, defined by Christ and not by sin. Sin in a believer is a sickness, a sickness he hates, but which draws out his compassion. In glory, Jesus' first reaction when you sin is pity. Where you would run *from* him in guilt, he would run *to* you in grace. It makes all the difference when your heart feels cold and cloddish. Right then you can know that your weary joylessness fills *him* with compassion.

The focus is upon Christ, but Goodwin was ardently trinitarian and could not abide the thought of his readers imagining a compassionate Christ appeasing a heartless Father. No, he said, "Christ adds not one drop of love to God's heart."[16] All Christ's tenderness comes in fact from the Spirit, who stirs him with the very love of the Father. The heart of Christ in heaven is the express image of the heart of his Father.

What Goodwin realized as a pastor was that this loving compassion is exactly what will draw us back to Christ from our sin. In our guilt we would never want to face up to some cold and pitiless God, but the tender kindness of Christ woos us. The beauty of Christ's heart in heaven wins ours. That certainly was the case for Goodwin himself, who said on his deathbed, "Christ cannot love me better than he doth. I think I cannot love Christ better than I do."[17]

My Advocate Is on High

The story of the Holy One ascending into God's presence wasn't a neglected curiosity for Old Testament Israel. In the very center of the land stood the Lord's "holy hill," complete with guardian cherubs. Today we call it the Temple Mount in Jerusalem; the Lord called it "Zion, my holy hill" (Ps 2:6 NIV 1984). There Solomon built a "dwelling place" for the Lord, decorated with golden cherubs (see 1 Kings 7–8). There in its innermost sanctuary the Lord was said to sit enthroned on the ark of the covenant. It was a symbolic replica of that original sanctuary of paradise on the holy hill of Mount Eden. And there was one man who, once a year, was allowed in there into the Lord's presence: the high priest. Part of his uniform was a gold plate tied to the front of his turban engraved with the words "HOLY TO THE LORD" (Ex 28:36). He was the Holy One, the only one with the right to enter the sanctuary.

Or at least, he was a picture of *the* Holy One. For the temple and all that went on in it was designed to be a picture, a teaching aid, telling us of heavenly reality. When at Mount Sinai Moses was first about to build the tabernacle, that original precursor to the temple, he was told to make it all "according to the pattern shown you on the mountain [where the LORD was]" (Ex 25:40). It meant that all those high priests in Jerusalem served as pictures of the heavenly High Priest, "at a sanctuary *that is a copy and shadow of what is in heaven*" (Heb 8:5).

With that in mind, picture the great events of the annual Day of Atonement, from Leviticus 16. Having sacrificed an animal for the sin of the people (representing the cross), the high priest would then take the blood of the sacrifice *behind the great veil, through into the Holy of Holies*, that innermost throne room of the Lord. Hebrews comments:

> When Christ came as high priest of the good things that are now already here, he went through the greater and more perfect tabernacle that is not made with human hands, that is to say, not a part of this creation. . . . For Christ did not enter a sanctuary made with human hands that was only a copy of the true one; he entered heaven itself, now to appear for us in God's presence. (Heb 9:11, 24)

In the ascension, Christ was serving as the true high priest, taking the actual blood of his own sacrifice to the very throne of God. And "when this priest had offered for all time one sacrifice for sins, he sat down at the right hand of God," his atoning work complete (Heb 10:12). *Complete.* Our firstborn brother in heaven, sitting down with nothing more to do with our sin. Finished. The unadulterated, happy security it gives each and every believer in Christ, weak or strong, means we can sing with hearts unshackled:

Before the throne of God above
I have a strong and perfect plea.
A great high Priest whose name is Love
Who ever lives and pleads for me.
My name is graven on His hands,
My name is written on His heart.
I know that while in Heaven He stands
No tongue can bid me thence depart.

When Satan tempts me to despair
And tells me of the guilt within,
Upward I look and see Him there
Who made an end of all my sin.
Because the sinless Savior died
My sinful soul is counted free.
For God the just is satisfied
To look on Him and pardon me.

Behold Him there the risen Lamb,
My perfect spotless righteousness,
The great unchangeable I AM,
The King of glory and of grace,
One in Himself I cannot die.
My soul is purchased by His blood,
My life is hid with Christ on high,
With Christ my Savior and my God![18]

And when our hearts are shackled and burdened, our great high priest still gives the dearest comfort. For there in heaven, filled with concern for the people he bled for, he pours out prayers into the ear of his loving Father.

Sadly, this sunny and radiant truth has been rather clouded over in Protestant circles. Fighting in the Reformation for the "priesthood of all believers" (that no men or women on earth stand as mediators between us and God), we have grown wary of the very word *priest*. The word can conjure in our minds a strange and frumpy creature dressed in the drawing-room curtains. But a common—and unnecessary—side-effect of this priestphobia is that we come to think that there is *no* mediator between us and God. Or if there is one, it's me. I stand on my own before God. And then the anxiety really kicks in.

Yet I do not stand on my own before God. I stand in Christ. I have a high priest who has atoned for me, and who on that basis now prays for me with total assurance. When I am faithless, he is faithful; when I am weak, he is strong; and when I can't even pray, he "is at the right hand of God and is also interceding for us" (Rom 8:34). Indeed, he lives to make intercession for us (Heb 7:25)! Our failings often make us hesitate to come to God; pain and heartache sometimes smash us so hard we simply don't have it in us to pray. It is at just such times that we can say with poor suffering Job,

> Even now my witness is in heaven;
>> my advocate is on high.
> My intercessor is my friend
>> as my eyes pour out tears to God;
> on behalf of a man he pleads with God
>> as one pleads for a friend. (Job 16:19-21)

Rise Up, O Lord! May Your Foes Flee Before You

So the high priests of Jerusalem were models of Christ in how they served. But there was something Jesus did in his ascension that no other high priest would have dared do—even in their earthly replica sanctuary. They had to fear even entering the place. But going into the true sanctuary, Christ then *sat down on the throne.*

It was no cheek: his Father commanded it.

> The LORD says to my lord:
> "Sit at my right hand
>> until I make your enemies
>> a footstool for your feet." (Ps 110:1)

Melchizedek offering bread and wine, from a sixth-century mosaic in Sant'Apollinare in Classe, Ravenna

For Christ was being a high priest of a whole different order: the order of Melchizedek, the priest-king of Jerusalem (Ps 110:4). Christ is our Melchizedek: both priest *and* king. And as king he has the right to sit down on the throne as the nations are made his inheritance, as every knee bows and every enemy is humbled before him.

"Who may ascend the mountain of the Lord?" asks Psalm 24. "Who may stand in his holy place?" We've heard the question before, but the answer given here is rather different:

Lift up your heads, O you gates;
    be lifted up, you ancient doors,
    that the King of glory may come in.
Who is this King of glory?
    The Lord strong and mighty,
    the Lord mighty in battle.
Lift up your heads, you gates;
    lift them up, you ancient doors,
    that the King of glory may come in.
Who is he, this King of glory?
    The Lord Almighty—
    he is the King of glory. (Ps 24:7-10)

The son of Mary, the adopted son of a carpenter, sits now on the throne of the universe. The victory he won on the cross is now paraded for all to see. He has disarmed the power of evil, and a man now stands, no longer a victim to the serpent's wiles, but a true king, utterly victorious. In him the psalm is fulfilled:

> What is man that you are mindful of him,
>   the son of man that you care for him?
> You made him a little lower than the heavenly beings
>   and crowned him with glory and honor.
> You made him ruler over the works of your hands;
>   you put everything under his feet:
> all flocks and herds,
>   and the beasts of the field,
> the birds of the air,
>   and the fish of the sea,
>   all that swim the paths of the seas. (Ps 8:4-8 NIV 1984)

This kingly triumph of Christ's would mean the fulfillment of what Adam was first created to be. When the first Adam was created, he was told: "Be fruitful and increase in number; *fill the earth* and subdue it" (Gen 1:28). But when Christ ascended, he "ascended higher than all the heavens, in order to *fill the whole universe*" with his life, his offspring and his glory (Eph 4:10; see also Col 1:6).

This is why the book of Acts—the book about the expansion of the church from Jerusalem to the ends of the earth—starts with the ascension of Christ. For Christ has been enthroned as king over all the earth, and his wonderful, life-giving reign must be proclaimed in all his territories. Going to his Father means his presence must be taken to the ends of the earth, for his kingdom extends from sea to sea. It is the ultimate stage of what he called his "lifting up": "I, when I am lifted up from the earth," he said, "will draw all people to myself" (Jn 12:32). Lifted up on the cross, lifted up from the grave, lifted up to the throne: all to share with the world his eternal and victorious life.

How it lifts our eyes! In the mundaneness of life, in failure, in sadness and in pain, we look up and find the deepest consolation.

There on the throne is death-crushing compassion and royal liberation: our friend, our priest, our king. The more we look, the more our hearts belong there, the more we want him known—and the more we long for his return.

4

Life in Christ

I Will Not Leave You as Orphans; I Will Come to You

Jesus went to heaven: it sounds glorious, but also rather sad. For we don't want him to go away; we want to be with him! Yet while he does go away from us *physically* in the ascension, our *relationship* with him only gets stronger after he goes to be with his Father. Thus he comforted his friends before it happened: "Do not let your hearts be troubled and do not be afraid. . . . If you loved me, you would be glad that I am going to the Father" (Jn 14:27-28).

Why? Because from heaven he would send his own Spirit—the Spirit of sonship—to unite us to himself, to make us one with him. Jesus had become one *of* us, but now by the

The Day of Pentecost by
Julius Schnorr von Carolsfeld, 1860

Spirit he would wonderfully become one *with* us. "For this is the design of the gospel," wrote John Calvin, "that Christ may become ours, and that we may be ingrafted into his body."[1] By the Spirit, said

Jesus, he and the Father would come and make their home with believers (Jn 14:23). "On that day you will realize that I am in my Father, *and you are in me, and I am in you*" (Jn 14:20).

The image Jesus used to explain all this, that night before his execution, was that of the Lord's Supper: "He [1] *took bread*, [2] *gave thanks* and [3] *broke it*, and [4] *gave it* to them, saying, 'This is my body given for you'" (Lk 22:19). Now if the bread is really all about his body, then in four little actions Jesus managed to encapsulate all that he was doing. He had come down from heaven and (1) *taken a body* as a man, and in that body he had lived a life of (2) *giving thanks* to God; he would then lay down that life, (3) *breaking his body* on the cross, all so that in the end, he could (4) *give himself* to us.

Jesus, then, does not have some loose affiliation with his people, some contract that depends on our faithfulness. Like the bread and wine we take into our bodies in Communion, he enters us by his Spirit and becomes *one* with us. In him, the divorce and division of sin is undone: the divorce between humanity and God, between person and person, between man and woman, black and white, Jew and Gentile. In him we are brought together and made *one*: one body, one loaf, one with each other and one with him:

> His purpose was to create in himself one new humanity out of the two [Jew and Gentile], thus making peace, and in one body to reconcile both of them to God through the cross, by which he put to death their hostility. He came and preached peace to you who were far away and peace to those who were near. For through him we both have access to the Father by one Spirit. (Eph 2:15-18)

To Love, Cherish and Obey

To speak of our oneness with Christ is really another way of speaking of Christ's marriage to his people. The bride and the Bridegroom have become one, and we are now together, for better, for worse, for richer, for poorer, in sickness and in health, till death, when we meet. And there can be no fear of a divorce here, for he has stated categorically: "I hate divorce" (Mal 2:16 NIV 1984).

Pause a moment. That utterly transforms what it means to be a Christian. For this marriage is no marriage of convenience. The point is not that we say "I do" to *use* him or his connections, simply to marry into his heavenly citizenship or status. We are not, as John Calvin put it, supposed to seek "in Christ something else than Christ himself."[2] The greatest benefit of union with Christ *is* Christ. This marriage is made so that we may know and enjoy *him*. Union with him is the foundation, *the beginning*: communion with him is the goal.

Take the apostle Paul as an example of one who felt this deep in his stomach. For all his obvious delight in justification by faith alone, salvation by grace alone, and so forth, his desire was not to depart and be *in heaven*. His hearty desire, he wrote to the Philippians, was to depart and be *with Christ* (Phil 1:23). Clearly, for him, heaven would not be heaven and salvation would not be salvation without Christ. That is the new heartbeat of the Christian: the Spirit opens our eyes to the glory and beauty of Christ that we might share the Father's eternal pleasure in him. "For God, who said, 'Let light shine out of darkness,' made his light shine in our hearts to give us the light of the knowledge of God's glory displayed in the face of Christ" (2 Cor 4:6). As God spoke light into darkness in creation, so his new creation means enlightening us to see the bright truth that Christ is gloriously desirable and valuable. Then—and only then!—do we think and feel straight, when the one preeminent in reality becomes preeminent in our thoughts, and the one eternally beloved of the Father becomes the beloved of all.

This all helps cut through one of those Christian debates that never die down. On the one hand, there are Christians who so want to emphasize the absolute freeness of salvation that any calls for holy living smack to them of attempts to earn God's favor. "Surely there can be no demands on us if salvation is truly free!" they cry. On the

other hand, you find a huge constituency quietly terrified of the
language of free salvation. "Don't tell people it's *completely* free!"
they murmur. "Else they'll never come to church or live holy lives."
As if "salvation" is some ethereal box of goodies received at death.

You can find the same tussle going on in church life between evan-
gelism and discipleship. At special evangelistic events people hear of
the free offer of salvation: "Get out of hell; heaven for free!" Who
wouldn't want that? So people sign up in droves. They're then deeply
puzzled by the discipleship classes: all the talk of holy living just doesn't
compute with the evangelistic message they heard. So they leave.

The mess goes away, though, if salvation *is* Christ. Then you cannot
separate salvation and Christian living—or justification and sanctifi-
cation—for both are about him, and he cannot be sliced up. God does
not have lumps of "righteousness" or "salvation" that he tears up and
lobs down from heaven. He has his righteous Son. So as a preacher I
offer *Christ* to all, completely free. But I offer no life apart from him.
He is salvation: *in* him is all righteousness and *knowing* him is the heart
of holiness. Martin Luther put it perfectly: "Through faith in Christ,"
he wrote, "Christ's righteousness becomes our righteousness and all
that he has becomes ours; *rather, He Himself becomes ours.*"[3] That is the
only reason we have his righteousness: because we have *him*. And
knowing him is the only life and liberty for which we are freely saved.

This also transforms what we *mean* by that tricky word *holiness*.
Anyone can use the word, of course, but without Christ *holiness* tends
to have all the charm of an ingrown toenail. For, very simply, if holiness
is not first and foremost about knowing Christ, it will be about self-
produced morality and religiosity. But such incurved self-dependence
is quite the opposite of what pleases God, or what is actually beautiful.
God is not interested in our manufactured virtue; he does not want any
external obedience or morality if it does not flow from true love for
him. He wants us to share his pleasure in his Son. What is the greatest
commandment, after all? "Love the Lord your God" (Mt 22:36-37).
That is the root of true God-likeness. Nothing is more holy than a

THE MERRY MESSENGER

Charles Spurgeon (1834–1892) was a phenomenon of the nineteenth century, a cataract bursting upon the world. As a man, he fizzed with life and good cheer; as a pastor, he was so fruitful he seems fictitious. Streams of living water flowed from within him. So what was the reservoir that fed him? Whence such verve and bounty?

The answer, without a doubt, is Jesus Christ. Christ was his treasure, his life, the organizing center of his thought and ministry. He had the highest view of Scripture, but he was not first and foremost a man of the Bible: his view of

Spurgeon preaching to a packed Surrey Music Hall, c. 1858

it and his use of it were steered by the fact that it is the word of *Christ*. He loved the Puritans, but he was not primarily a Puritan out of time: he went to them as heralds of *Christ*. He was an avowed Calvinist, but not for the sake of a system in itself: he embraced whatever theology he saw most glorifying *Christ*.

In his first sermon in the Metropolitan Tabernacle, on March 25, 1861, he said, "I would propose that the subject of the ministry of this house, as long as this platform shall stand, and as long as this house shall be frequented by worshippers, shall be the person of Jesus Christ."[4] And he did not stray from that in the thirty years he pastored there. These are his last ever words from the pulpit, dated June 1891:

It is heaven to serve Jesus. I am a recruiting sergeant, and
I would fain find a few recruits at this moment. Every man
must serve somebody: we have no choice as to that fact.
Those who have no master are slaves to themselves. De-
pend upon it, you will either serve Satan or Christ, either
self or the Savior. You will find sin, self, Satan, and the
world to be hard masters; but if you wear the livery of
Christ, you will find him so meek and lowly of heart that
you will find rest unto your souls. He is the most mag-
nanimous of captains. There never was his like among the
choicest of princes. He is always to be found in the thick-
est part of the battle. When the wind blows cold he always
takes the bleak side of the hill. The heaviest end of the
cross lies ever on his shoulders. If he bids us carry a burden, he carries it also. If there is anything that is gracious,
generous, kind, and tender, yea lavish and superabundant
in love, you always find it in him. These forty years and
more have I served him, blessed be his name! and I have
had nothing but love from him. I would be glad to continue yet another forty years in the same dear service here
below if so it pleased him. His service is life, peace, joy.
Oh, that you would enter on it at once! God help you to
enlist under the banner of Jesus even this day! Amen.[5]

In those words you see it: he preached *Christ*. Not some abstract gospel with an abstract reward of "grace" or "heaven." He
preached *Christ*. And, you can see, he *preached* Christ. Those
are not the words of a lecturer, merely filling minds with information; those are the words of a herald issuing a summons.
That is how it must be if the new life of the believer is about
oneness with Christ. Before all else, the Bride needs to hear of
the Bridegroom, of how good he is and how winning his love.

heartfelt delight in Christ. Nothing is so powerful to transform lives.

But how can we, without hypocrisy, come to embrace Christ as our most dearly cherished treasure? Only when we sense his unfathomable love for us, how kind and merciful he is and has been, how much he has suffered for our forgiveness, how he is truly better than all the other things we run after. We love him because he first loved us (1 Jn 4:19). In other words, what all my efforts could not achieve, the love of Christ achieves: it wins me to love God and love others with sincerity, freedom and spontaneity. I begin to *enjoy* holiness and *hate* sin because I enjoy him and hate what stands against him in all his goodness, truth and beauty.

Jesus himself put it startlingly: "The kingdom of heaven has been forcefully advancing, and forceful men lay hold of it" (Mt 11:12 NIV 1984). That is, the very violence of God's grace—his driving out of demons and his determination to die for us—fills us with a corresponding violence of passion for him. A mighty wind comes upon his people and they are filled with fire. The very fierceness, the fury of his love toward us consumes our natural lethargy toward him, and we begin—forcefully!—to *want* him.

The Life of the Son

There is so much more to savor here. For our union with Christ means not only that he is the Bridegroom of his people, the one we love; he is also our head, the firstborn among us. That is, we not only come to share the Father's pleasure in him; we come to share the life he enjoys before the Father. We stand in him with his own unspotted confidence before his Father—and there the Spirit draws us to live out his life and sonship. That is why he lived and died in our place, that we might live (and die) in his.

The Son's very identity is found in this: that he is the beloved of the Father. All that he does flows from that identity. He does not act out of guilt, neediness or a desire to curry favor with his Father or anyone else. For eternity, his Father has showered him with so much love that he overflows. He cannot but love his Father back, and long to please him. Being the Son of so perfectly kind a Father, it is meat and drink for him to do his will (Jn 4:34). That is the life of the Son of God.

And that is the life we are drawn into. Just as the Father has always poured out the Spirit of his love upon his dear Son, so now "God's love has been poured out into *our hearts* through the [same] Holy Spirit" (Rom 5:5). Paul wrote in Romans that "those who are led by the Spirit of God are children of God. The Spirit you received does not make you slaves, so that you live in fear again; rather, the Spirit you received brought about your adoption to sonship. And by him we cry, 'Abba, Father'" (Rom 8:14-15). Christians do not receive a spirit of slavery and fear, of desperate insecurity before God. We can slip into thinking that way and lose our peace and joy, but that is not the life to which we have been called. Believers receive the very Spirit of the Son, *and he wakes us up to share the holy tastes of the Son.* I begin to cry out to God like I've never cried out before: I call him my *Abba*, my dear Father.

WHOLEHEARTED

Caleb is one of my favorite Old Testament characters, and the only one repeatedly said to have followed the Lord fully or wholeheartedly. We first get to meet him when he is sent by Moses to reconnoiter Canaan as one of the twelve Israelite spies. He is described then as being "from the tribe of Judah, Caleb son of Jephunneh" (Num 13:6). So we know two things about him: he is of the tribe of Judah, and his father is Jephunneh.

So far, so easy. But later in Numbers he is called "Caleb son of Jephunneh *the Kenizzite*" (Num 32:12), the Kenizzites being one of those scary tribes of *pagan* Canaanites (Gen 15:19). So Caleb is an ethnic Gentile, not a native Jew. Almost certainly that explains his name, for Caleb means "dog" in Hebrew, and the Israelites commonly referred to foreigners as "Gentile dogs." Like Rahab, Ruth and many others, a Gentile "dog" had joined Israel and been adopted into the royal tribe of Judah. Though born a pagan, he would receive an inheritance as a part of Judah (Josh 15:13). Indeed, of all the wilderness generation, it was only Joshua and Caleb who survived to enter the land: an ethnic Jew and an ethnic Gentile walking together and equal into God's reward.

Joshua and Caleb carry the firstfruits of the Promised Land (Num 13:23)

Is it a coincidence that Caleb was repeatedly spoken of as wholehearted for the Lord? Surely not. He had been adopted, welcomed and embraced, and found he *belonged* with the Lord and his people. He was far less likely to fall into Baal worship, and remained a lionhearted soldier of the Lord into his late eighties. Adoption is a powerful and heart-affecting thing. It was for Caleb as a son of Judah; it is for us as children of God. We have been shown such kindness, and now we belong with our Father.

The Spirit of adoption brings me to share the Son's own affection for his Father, and for the first time I fulfill what I was made for: I love the Lord my God. Like Christ, I find I *want* to be with him, I *want* to pour out my heart to him, I *want* to please him and find my rest in him.

The love that the Father pours out on the Son by the Spirit is *expansive*: it moves the Son not only to cherish his Father but also to share his Father's outgoing concerns. Thus Jesus made Isaiah 61:1-2 the manifesto for his ministry:

> The Spirit of the Lord is on me,
>   because he has anointed me
>   to proclaim good news to the poor.
> He has sent me to proclaim freedom for the prisoners
>   and recovery of sight for the blind,
> to set the oppressed free,
>   to proclaim the year of the Lord's favor. (Lk 4:18-19)

Energized and empowered by the Spirit, the Son goes out, bringing the blessing, liberty and healing of his life-giving Father.

And once again, so it is for those in Christ. That is the life the children of God are called into. With hearts filled by the love of the Father, with an energy that comes from the Spirit and not themselves, they share the compassion of the Son and his pity for the weak and the lost. The Spirit remolds us so that we begin to find the Son's own joy in being like our Father, with his concern for the world. It is the new heartbeat of the children of God: sharing the joys, the passions, the heart cries and the concerns of the Son. And entirely unlike our natural heartbeat of flesh, which grows ever weaker, this grows only stronger as the Spirit breathes into us the life eternal.

Take how it is with sin. We died to sin, says Paul in Romans 6:2. We died with Christ, and we were raised in him to a new life. That is objective fact. It doesn't always *feel* true, given how much sin still lingers! But as the Spirit so kindly works in me, I begin to enjoy that truth subjectively as well, in my daily experience. The more I know myself to be a true child of God, and the more I see of Christ, the deader I find myself to sin. It still allures me, but not as it did. I find old sinful desires dying and new holy ones springing up: I find myself longing, *yearning* to be free of the sins I once held so dearly. I have a new heart, after all—the heart of a child of God— and it feels and wants differently. Like Christ. In fact, in all I am a new creation: I have new ears that hear differently, a new brain that thinks differently, new hands that act differently and a new tongue that speaks differently.

There is a beautiful moment in Hebrews 2 that visually captures this sharing of the Son's life. There, in a quotation from Psalm 22, we read of Jesus saying to God, "In the midst of the congregation I will sing your praise" (Heb 2:12 ESV; Ps 22:22). You can picture it: there he is, the firstborn, surrounded by his brothers and sisters, the children of God; and there in the congregation of the saints he leads our praise. He is our ultimate worship leader (see also Mt 26:30; Rom 15:9). He stands at the front, singing God's praises. And we sing along. He says, "I will put my trust in him" (Heb 2:13; Is 8:17), and we all roar "Amen!"

It is a snapshot of the whole relationship between the firstborn and the ones he says he is not ashamed to call brothers and sisters (Heb 2:11). He delights to do the will of his Father, and (slowly!) as the Spirit works, we come to share his delight. There at the front, he is a king, victorious over the world, the flesh and the devil, and behind him we share his victory, watching sin steadily trampled under our feet, waiting for Satan finally to be crushed there. He is a priest, interceding for his people and the world, and we put our hands by his and pray with him. He is a prophet, making his Father known to the world, and we join his mission.

What a far cry this is from the exhausting idea that Christ has done his bit and now it's time to do ours! We are not chained to the task of trying to pay back the huge debt we owe him. We are united to the Son so we can enter into his life. Our joy, our prayers, our mission, our holiness, our suffering, our hope: all are a *participation* in the life of the Son. We are not simply given some *thing* called "eternal life" and then sent out to get on with it. We are not forerunners with final responsibility. He is the firstborn; we live in his slipstream.

It means as you go through life, you can have the relief of knowing that you are not on your own, facing a list of tasks.

Whatever you do, you are not the indispensable one. You are simply entering into the life of the Son, sharing his agonies, his concerns, his passions and his joys. With him.

We Rejoice in Our Sufferings

We must suffer. That much is plain if the life we are brought to share is the life of Christ. "Dear friends, do not be surprised at the fiery ordeal that has come on you to test you, as though something strange were

happening to you," wrote Peter. "But rejoice inasmuch as you participate in the sufferings of Christ, so that you may be overjoyed when his glory is revealed" (1 Pet 4:12-13). He is the firstborn, our forerunner, and where he goes, we follow. As the Israelites trailed behind the ark of the covenant through the wilderness and into Canaan, so we walk in his footsteps. Through suffering to glory. Therefore we cannot simply read suffering as a sign that our Father does not care. Far, far

Simon of Cyrene takes up Christ's cross, from Duccio's *Maestà*, 1311

from it. Instead, remember that word of encouragement that addresses you as sons:

> My son, do not make light of the Lord's discipline,
> and do not lose heart when he rebukes you,
> because the Lord disciplines those he loves. (Heb 12:5-6;
>   quoting Prov 3:11-12)

It is not that all our suffering is the consequence of specific acts of ours for which we need disciplining (though sometimes it might be!). The point is that God uses even suffering for our ultimate blessing. He did just that at the cross: it was through that darkest day, that deepest pit of suffering, that he definitively overturned and defeated the very root of darkness and suffering. Through that death he defeated death; through our *comparatively* light sufferings he is able to defeat our selfish independence and our foolish wandering and make us more like his free and victorious Son. For those who have glimpsed the unfettered beauty of Jesus, that thought itself puts mettle in our joy. For having seen in him what it looks like to be free of sin's shriveling power, we want to be like him! Thus in Acts 5, when Peter and the apostles were flogged before the Sanhedrin, they left "rejoicing because they had been counted worthy of suffering disgrace for the Name" (the dear name of Jesus). It wasn't that the flogging didn't hurt. It was that their desire to be like Jesus was stronger. There was joy to be found in participating in the sufferings of Christ.

In Peter we see two things that cannot be explained or understood by the world. First, the pattern of suffering followed by glory. Second, and more astounding, that does *not* mean suffering *and only then* joy. No, for Christ and his people, joy precedes, follows, undermines and encases all suffering. Christ had joy *before* all pain, before the world existed (see echoes of this in Proverbs 8:30). And it was joy that strengthened his resolve then to suffer (Heb 12:2). That is what he shares with us: a preceding joy that enables us to bear hardship. It is the happy secret of the saints who have borne suffering most cheerfully and bravely for Christ: the more we find our pleasure in him, the more willing we will then be to suffer with him. As Richard Sibbes put it:

> We cannot please Christ better than in shewing our selves welcome, by cheerful taking part of his rich provision. It is an honour to his bounty to fall to; and it is the temper of spirit that a Christian aims at, to "rejoice always in the Lord," Phil.

iv. 4. . . . What will we do for him, if we will not feast with him? *We will not suffer with him, if we will not feast with him; we will not suffer with him, if we will not joy with him, and in him.*[6]

It means that, if Christians are to cope with and even rejoice in the suffering we will face, *before anything else we need to hear about Jesus.* We need our eyes filled with the glory of Christ—how all-satisfying he is—so that we love him and want him. Only then will we actually *rejoice* in our sufferings, because only then will we want that much to be like him.

Bruised . . . and Bruising

Just as suffering in Christ is set about on all sides by joy, so it is surrounded and conditioned by the most buoyant hope. Take the very first time the suffering of Christ is mentioned in Scripture, when the Lord says to the serpent,

I will put enmity
between you and the woman,
and between your offspring and hers;
he will crush your head,
and you will strike his heel. (Gen 3:15)

That, of course, tells us about Christ: *the* promised Son, *the* offspring of the woman. But the apostle Paul believed that it could also then be applied to all who are *in* Christ: "The God of peace will soon crush Satan under *your* feet," he wrote (Rom 16:20). For Christians are those who have been brought into Christ, who is both the bruised one *and* the one who bruises.

United to the bruised one, Christians enter into a particular life of suffering. Harassed by Satan, opposed by the world and increasingly unhappy with the sin inside that we once loved, Christians face more than the ordinary pains of life. But. Yes, *but.* Not only are we bound for glory, as surely as Christ himself; *even as we are bruised now*, with our great firstborn brother we do some bruising! Every time you rejoice in Christ, resist sin, proclaim him and show his love, you press home the victory of Christ. You stamp on the serpent's head. That is the bigger perspective of Scripture: never triumphalistic, but definitely triumphant. Satan nibbles at our feet; we crush his head. "We are hard pressed on every side, but not crushed; perplexed, but not in despair; persecuted, but not abandoned; struck down, but not destroyed. We always carry around in our body the death of Jesus, so that the life of Jesus may also be revealed in our body" (2 Cor 4:8-10).

An Identity Before All Others

What I am trying to say in this chapter, really, is simply this: our union with Christ is not just the appetizer to the Christian life, the soup we push back as we wait for the meat to arrive. It is not the doorway that leads us through into a life that is about *something else*. It *is* the steak and the living room of the Christian life.

Yet how easily we shuffle on elsewhere! For me, I find the weight of what I do with my time, the sheer allotment of my hours, makes me think I *am* what I do. And quietly I come to think of myself primarily not as a son of God in Christ but as successful or unsuccessful, popular or unpopular—depending on how the day's going. Bluntly, when not defined by Christ, I find myself as fragile as a puffed-up balloon. When I begin to define myself by success or popularity, they matter far too much to me: when I get them, my ego inflates preposterously; when I don't, I implode. That simply can't happen when the core of my identity is consciously found in Christ, for he is the same—yesterday, today and forever.

It's not just for our own personal sanity: when Christians define themselves by something other than Christ, they poison the air all round. When they crave power and popularity, and they get it, they become pompous, patronizing or simply bullies. And when they don't get it, they become bitter, apathetic or prickly. Whether flushed by success or burnt by lack of it, both have cared too much for the wrong thing. Defining themselves by something other than Christ, they become like something other than Christ. Ugly.

Our union with Christ thus has deep plough work to do in our hearts. It automatically and immediately gives us a new *status*, but for that status and identity to be *felt* to be the deepest truth about

I AM THE VINE; YOU ARE THE BRANCHES

"I am the vine; you are the branches." It boggles the mind just how much work that simple image does. There it is: our union and our communion with Christ. He is the vine; we are the branches (Jn 15:1-8). One. In vital, closest union. No distance. The vine holds nothing back from its branches, pouring all its life into them.

It makes the nature of the Christian life so easy to see. There can be *no* life or true fruitfulness apart from him (verse 5). On our own we are but withered sticks. Which knocks the wind out of you if you think of yourself as strong and capable. For what can all your brilliance, determination and oomph achieve? Precisely nothing. Or nothing *positive*, in any case, apart from him. It means we do not try to produce fruit *in order to join the vine, or to stay in it*; we bear fruit *when we receive the life of the vine*. Our part is to remain there. Then the fertile sap of the Spirit will flow through us, producing fruit.

And there the vinedresser, our Father, will prune us, making us even more fruitful (verse 2). What a comfort this is for the suffering believer! For the picture is not of some pie-eyed oaf, greedily slashing at his vine to get a bigger harvest for his cellar. The vinedresser is the Father; the vine his dear Son. Think of the pain Jesus felt when Saul was persecuting his people: "Saul, Saul, why do you persecute *me*?" he asked (Acts 9:4). The Father would make no callous cut here; but to liberate his people from all that enslaves them and makes them fruit-less—to bring us the full life of the vine—he will lovingly prune.

So our part is simply to remain? It sounds so passive, so at odds with Paul, always fighting the good fight and running the race (2 Tim 4:7). But when Jesus unpacks what it means, it is clear that "to remain" does not mean "to be inert." It means: have "my words remain in you" (verse 7); and it means "remain in my love" (verse 9). There is the center ground of the Christian fight: to have the gospel of Christ's love as our sap and food. It means being full of Scripture, ignorance of Scripture being ignorance of Christ. But it means much more than that as well. Jesus said to those who "study the Scriptures diligently" (Jn 5:39) that God's word did *not* remain in them "for you do not *believe* the one he sent" (Jn 5:38). It means, then, that we come to Scripture with a purpose: to know Christ, to love and trust him and to come to him for life (Jn 5:40). It means hearing him proclaimed by others, singing of him, enjoying him through his creation as the author and model of beauty, and savoring his aroma in acts of love and kindness. Then the fruit will come.

There's just one bit that worries people here: the Father "cuts off every branch in me that bears no fruit" (Jn 15:2). Does that mean that if you don't pull your weight as a Christian you get "picked up, thrown into the fire and burned" (verse 6)? No, true branches that have a living connection to the vine are *never* cut off. Jesus said earlier that

> This is the will of him who sent me, that I shall lose none of all that he has given me, but raise them up at the last day. For my Father's will is that everyone who looks to the Son and believes in him shall have eternal life, and I will raise him up at the last day. (Jn 6:39-40)

> I give them eternal life, and they shall never perish; no one can snatch them out of my hand. (Jn 10:28)

Jesus gave his disciples the image of the vine while in the upper room, the night before he died. *Judas had just left to betray him.* In that context, the point was clear: there are some who spend time

among God's people who eventually prove that Christ's love was
never their sap and food. Having no sap in them, of course they
don't bear fruit. In other words, those dead branches are not weak,
backsliding *believers*. They are those who eventually prove that they
never had a living connection to the vine.

Believers are meant to know assurance. "I write these things to you
who believe in the name of the Son of God so that you may *know* that
you have eternal life," wrote John (1 Jn 5:13). And if you still remain
worried about whether or not you belong in the vine, simply come
now to Christ. "Whoever comes to me I will never drive away," he says
(Jn 6:37). Come to Christ, and know it is not your feelings of faithfulness that keep you safe in him, but his loving and almighty embrace.

ourselves is a radical, ongoing business. That is the primary identity
of the believer, though, and the only foundation for truly Christian
living. For our health, joy and fellowship, then, we must take up
arms against the insidious idea that we have any identity—
background, ability or status—more basic than that of sharing the
Son's own life together before the Father.

Make Your Face Shine Upon Us, That We May Be Saved

Since, then, Christ is our life, the one we are brought to enjoy and
the one in whom we live and move and have our being, he must be
the secret or mystery of godliness. "Beyond all question," wrote Paul,
"the mystery from which true godliness springs is great." He goes on:

> He appeared in the flesh,
> was vindicated by the Spirit,
> was seen by angels,
> was preached among the nations,
> was believed on in the world,
> was taken up in glory. (1 Tim 3:16)

It's not a technique, a method or a habit. The essential secret of godliness is Christ. Sin is precisely Christlessness; all attempts at self-improvement and moral reformation without him are sin. Only through knowing and relying on him can we become like the living God and share his vitality.

It means that before anything else it matters where we *look*. Before anything else it matters what fills our vision. For whatever it is that occupies our attention (or, to use Jesus' words, whatever it is that "remains" in us), that will steer and shape our every thought, motive and action. *You are what you see.* Michel Foucault noticed this when he was looking at the use of the confessional in Roman Catholicism. After the Reformation of the sixteenth century, as Rome sought to put its house in order, the practice of confessing your sins to a priest became ever more strongly encouraged. Through acknowledging and confessing their sinfulness, it was thought, people would be spurred on to deeper holiness. What actually happened, Foucault observed, was that people only came to identify themselves more strongly *as sinners*. Sure, the priest had uttered his absolution, but the whole practice *put the focus on the sin* being confessed. Through that prolonged *look*, they bound themselves tighter to the very things they sought to escape. (None of that is to suggest that self-examination itself is a bad thing, of course; it is simply that a *focus on self* is not the secret of godliness.)

Peter looked at the wind and began to sink (Mt 14:29-30)

Life, righteousness, holiness and redemption are found in Jesus, and found by those—and only those!—who *look* to him. Perhaps I should be clearer: it is not that we look, get some sense of what Christ is like, and then go away and strain to make ourselves

similar; we become like him *through the very looking*. The very sight
of him is a transforming thing. For now, contemplating him by faith,
we begin to be transformed into his likeness (2 Cor 3:18), but so
potent is his glory that when we clap eyes upon him physically at
his second coming, then "we shall be like him, *for we shall see him
as he is*" (1 Jn 3:2). That full, unveiled, physical sight of the glorified
Jesus will be so majestically effecting it will transform our very
bodies around us. The sight of him now by the Spirit makes us
more like him spiritually; the sight of him then, face to face, will
finally make us—body and soul—as he is. Contemplating Christ
now is thus rather like seeing the morning star at the break of day:
both enchanting and full of hope. It is light for now with the
promise of so much more to come. It is a taste of heaven.

The language of light is quite appropriate, for the sight of Jesus
is like the eruption of glorious light into darkness: it illumines our
minds, it makes our faces shine and it drives away our darkness. It
is grace, and it is gracious judgment. The light of his perfection
exposes our imperfection more than any wielding of the law ever
could. It makes us see ourselves aright. As John Calvin put it, "man
never achieves a clear knowledge of himself unless he has first
looked upon God's face."[7] But it does more than expose: it *over-
comes* our imperfection and so liberates us. And once again, it cures
us far more effectively than any effort at self-improvement. Like the
genial sun on the frost of our hearts, said Charles Spurgeon:

> I cannot liken it to anything that I know of better than the snow
> which melts in the sun. You wake up one morning, and all the
> trees are festooned with snowy wreaths, while down below
> upon the ground the snow lies in a white sheet over everything.
> Lo, the sun has risen, its beams shed a genial warmth; and in a
> few hours where is the snow? It has passed away. *Had you hired
> a thousand carts and horses and machines to sweep it away it
> could not have been more effectually removed.* It has passed away.

That is what the Lord does in the new creation: His love shines
on the soul, His grace renews us, and the old things pass away
as a matter of course. . . . Where His blessed face beams with
grace and truth, as the sun with warmth and light, He dissolves
the bands of sin's long frost, and brings on the spring of grace
with newness of buds and flowers.[8]

Or, as Paul phrased it, "The grace of God has appeared that offers
salvation to all people. *It* teaches us to say 'No' to ungodliness and
worldly passions" (Tit 2:11-12). That is, it is the very grace of God,
appearing from heaven in Christ, that turns hearts from worldly
passions to godly passions. Where self-dependent efforts at self-
improvement must leave us self-obsessed and therefore fundamen-
tally unloving, the kindness of God in Christ attracts our hearts
away from ourselves *to him*. Only the love of Christ has this power
to uncoil a human heart.

Now if that is the case, there seems to be a worrying hole in
modern Christianity. Our helter-skelter lives keep our eyes *down*
and away from Christ. Professor David Bebbington has argued that
one of the four defining marks of the evangelical is *activism*, and he
was probably right. Indeed, you don't have to self-identify as an
evangelical to know yourself an activist. But while activism itself is
no bad thing (Christians, after all, are people on a mission), it is
fraught with the tendency to self-dependence. It is no great wonder
that burnout is so common a feature of the Christian landscape.

What to do? We could keep our eyes down and recommend better
time management, more rounded lives and so forth, but they would
be mere palliatives, staving off the ultimate breakdown. No, the *root*
of our spiritual exhaustion must be dealt with. Here is Dr. John
Owen's prescription:

Do any of us find decays in grace prevailing in us;—deadness,
coldness, lukewarmness, a kind of spiritual stupidity and
senselessness coming upon us? . . . Let us assure ourselves

> there is no better way for our healing and deliverance, yea, no
> other way but this alone,—namely, the obtaining a fresh view
> of the glory of Christ by faith, and a steady abiding therein.
> Constant contemplation of Christ and his glory, putting forth
> its transforming power unto the revival of all grace, is the only
> relief in this case.[9]

In fact, Owen had discovered that contemplating Christ was more
powerful even than that. Owen was a man tragically familiar with
heartbreak. At one point, in the 1650s, he was the vice-chancellor
of Oxford University, successful and influential, but in the second
half of his life he was pushed into obscurity and social exile, ham-
pered and harassed by the new government. Heavily outweighing
all that, he had to witness the burial of all eleven of his children, as
well as his wife, Mary. After the death of the first ten children, he
wrote these words: "a due contemplation of the glory of Christ will
restore and compose the mind. . . . [It] will lift the minds and hearts
of believers above all the troubles of this life, and is the sovereign
antidote that will expel all the poison that is in them; which
otherwise might perplex and enslave their souls."[10]

Death, sin, sadness, slavery, despair: in Christ there is antidote
for it all.

5

Come, Lord Jesus!

This Same Jesus

Every fiftieth year in Israel was supposed to be a year of jubilee, a year of liberty and rest. In that year, debts would be canceled, slaves freed, and the people and the very land itself would be allowed to rest: no sowing or reaping would be done. It was to be a foretaste of the Bible's cosmic hope: the time when all our debt will be canceled, when our captivity and bondage to decay and evil will be ended, when the meek will inherit the earth.

Here's how it would be inaugurated:

> Count off seven sabbath years—seven times seven years—so that the seven sabbath years amount to a period of forty-nine years. Then have the trumpet sounded everywhere on the tenth day of the seventh month; *on the Day of Atonement sound the trumpet* throughout your land. Consecrate the fiftieth year and proclaim liberty throughout the land to all its inhabitants. It shall be a jubilee for you. (Lev 25:8-10)

So the high priest would make atonement, and *that* would usher in this era of peace. He would take the sacrificial blood into the Holy of Holies and sprinkle it on the mercy seat, and when he was done and he stepped back out to prove it, *then* the trumpet would sound, proclaiming rest to all the land. To anyone who has read the New Testament, it all sounds rather familiar: the sounding of the trumpet, announcing the atonement-bought goal of all things (1 Cor 15:52; 1 Thess 4:16). And it should sound familiar, for just as the high priest's *going in* to the Holy of Holies was a picture of Christ's ascension to heaven, so the high priest's *return* was a picture of Christ's. Especially in the jubilee year: atonement made, he returns, the trumpet sounds, and all is jubilee.

That little detail about the high priest's return carries a truckload of comfort: the man who stepped into the Holy of Holies is *the very same man* who steps back out. It means, as the angels told the gawking disciples, that *"this same Jesus,* who has been taken from you into heaven, will come back in the same way you have seen him go into heaven" (Acts 1:11). When the trumpet sounds and the Judge of all the earth appears, we will see our firstborn brother, the same one who died to make atonement for us. The Heidelberg Catechism puts the issue directly, asking, "What *comfort* is it to you that Christ will come to judge the living and the dead?" (The very wording is so affecting: not "How terrifying is that thought?" but "What comfort is it to you?") The correct answer for all who trust him is this irresistible reply:

In all my sorrow and persecution
I lift up my head
and eagerly await
as judge from heaven
the very same person
who before has submitted himself
to the judgement of God
for my sake,
and has removed all the curse from me.[1]

Those words sing the theology of the Reformation. In medieval Roman Catholicism, the need to have your own personal merit before God left people with almost no comfort in the thought that Christ will return. You can feel the undiluted terror his return inspired when you see medieval frescoes of the Last Judgment, which show the naked dead seized by grotesque demons and forced into the fire. You hear it in the words of the *Dies Irae* that were chanted in every Catholic Mass for the Dead: "Day of wrath, day that will dissolve the world into burning coals. . . . What am I the wretch then to say? what patron I to beseech? when scarcely the just be secure. King of tremendous Majesty . . . do not lose me on that day. . . . My prayers are not worthy, but do Thou, Good [God], deal kindly lest I burn in perennial fire."

Of course, if Christ is not really one with us—if he leaves us, unconnected to himself, somehow to win our own personal destiny—that is how I must view that day. Anything else would be the most hubristic presumption. But if Christ is our forerunner, our head, the bridegroom who went only to prepare a place for his bride, then that day is no longer simply the Doomsday. It is what Martin Luther called "the most happy Last Day."[2] For as surely as Christ is in glory, his own must join him. The head cannot have glory without the body. The Bridegroom will not keep what is his to himself. Christians can therefore confidently long for that day as the time when we will sing,

> Let us rejoice and be glad
> and give him glory!
> For the wedding of the Lamb has come. (Rev 19:7)

The judge of all the earth is the one who bled for us.

The Lamb Is Its Lamp

He is the center and spring of all our future hope. Indeed, any hope that has another focus or essence is not essentially Christian. We pray, "Your kingdom come"; we long for our captivity to sin and decay to be over; but the heart of the church's hope is the bride's wish to be with the Bridegroom, face to face (Rev 22:17). Central to the great promises of God is this: "I will live with them" (see Lev 26:12; Ezek 37:27; 2 Cor 6:16; Rev 21:3). Christians are those who eagerly wait for "the blessed hope—the appearing of the glory of our great God and Savior,

The Adoration of the Lamb by Albrecht Dürer, c. 1498

Jesus Christ" (Tit 2:13; see also 1 Thess 1:10). "*Maranatha!* Come, Lord Jesus," we cry, for heaven would not be heaven without him (1 Cor 16:22; Rev 22:20).

It is not that he is *all that will matter*, as if the final conquest of evil and the resurrection of our bodies were trifling things; he is the center in that he is the *fountainhead and source* of all the blessings of the new creation. He is the light that drives away the darkness; he is the life that defeats death; "he is the beginning and the firstborn from among the dead" (Col 1:18). But it is precisely by having him as our focus then that we will enjoy the blessings he brings. We will find ourselves transformed, freed from sin and physically perfected, becoming like him because "*we shall see him as he is*" (1 Jn 3:2). And then the creation "will be liberated from its bondage to decay and brought into the freedom and glory of the children of God" (Rom 8:21). Individual transformation and cosmic renewal—all because Jesus will have complete primacy, with every knee bowing to him. For now, sin makes all things eccentric; round Jesus, all things will find what they are meant to be.

The Winter of Our Discontent Made Glorious Summer

This righting and reordering of creation is put most strikingly by Psalm 98:

> Shout for joy to the LORD, all the earth,
>   burst into jubilant song with music;
> make music to the LORD with the harp,

with the harp and the sound of singing,
with trumpets and the blast of the ram's horn—
shout for joy before the LORD, the King.

Let the sea resound, and everything in it,
the world, and all who live in it.
Let the rivers clap their hands,
let the mountains sing together for joy;
let them sing before the LORD,
for he comes to judge the earth. (Ps 98:4-9)

The earth rejoices *because* he comes to judge it! Why? Because, as we saw in his first coming, this one does not judge like any other. Utterly just and good, his judgment is all about removing evil, wickedness and injustice. Today, the creation groans under the weight of our sin, with all its piled-up death and cruelty; his judgment means liberation.

It is as it was before Joshua took the people into the Promised Land. The foul depravity of the Canaanites—showcased in their willingness to burn their sons and daughters as sacrifices to the gods—made the very land retch at their presence (Lev 18:25). The sounding of the ram's horn trumpets at Jericho thus meant a judgment that was deliverance: the perpetrators would be removed for the healing of a land the people of God could inherit. Just so, our Jesus is the true Joshua (Jesus is the Greek form of the Hebrew name Joshua) who comes to cleanse the earth for his people. That is why the creation waits in eager expectation for that day, for his judgment does not mean the destruction of the *creation* once declared good; it means the destruction of all *evil* for the *renewal* of the creation. Terrible news for evil and those who cling to it, to be sure; but pure joy for those who embrace him.

The principal image used in Scripture to show the utter goodness of Christ's judgment is that of light confronting night. In the very beginning, God speaks light. Then we are told *not* "there was morning then evening" but "there was *evening* and *then* morning."

Each day thus testifies to the grand story of reality, that light will follow darkness and defeat it (a lesson entirely lost by reckoning each day from midnight to midnight instead of dusk to dusk). As John would put it when he came to describe this Word: "The light shines in the darkness, and the darkness has not overcome it" (Jn 1:5).

This judgment has in fact already started at the house of God, with those who are in Christ. Right now, the light begins the work of driving away the gloomy night of our sin: "For God, who said, 'Let light shine out of darkness,' made his light shine in our hearts to give us the light of the knowledge of God's glory displayed in the face of Christ" (2 Cor 4:6). This is a kind judgment indeed! Our devilish darkness dispelled by the light of Christ. And it all climaxes in the eternal summer of the new Jerusalem, when the Light of the world will have driven away all darkness: "There will be no more night. They will not need the light of a lamp or the light of the sun, for the Lord God will give them light. And they will reign for ever and ever" (Rev 22:5).

The Lion Who Is a Lamb

Perhaps even more unexpected than the goodness of Christ in his judgment is the *nature* of the sovereign power that he wields to judge. Think how it is expressed, again and again, in the book of Revelation. We are told that a sacrificed *Lamb* is triumphant and all-powerful to judge. He is able and worthy to open the great scroll of destiny that will determine the judgment of the world

> *because* you were slain,
> and with your blood you purchased for God
> persons from every tribe and language and people and
> nation. (Rev 5:9)

That is no throwaway line: John clearly wants us to think on the self-sacrificial, self-giving nature of the Lamb's power, and rarely strays far from the theme. The Lamb conquers *through his self-giving*.

It is shown in sharp relief when the Lamb is contrasted with various other figures in the book that people are drawn to worship. The dragon, for instance. Like the Lamb, the dragon is a powerful, crowned and many-horned being; *unlike* the Lamb, the dragon wants only to devour (Rev 12:4). Where the Lamb has *suffered* death for others, the dragon only seeks to *inflict* death on others. The one gives *out* life; the other sucks *in* life. Or think of the beasts in Revelation 13, who in many ways are sick parodies of

"They triumphed over him by the blood of the Lamb" (Rev 12:11)

the Lamb. One beast "seemed to have had a fatal wound, but the fatal wound had been healed" (Rev 13:3). Fatally wounded, yet alive. Rather like the Lamb. The other beast is directly said to be *"like a lamb*, but it spoke like a dragon" (Rev 13:11). As the power of God is exercised through the Lamb, the power of the dragon is exercised through the beasts (Rev 13:2). But once again, how different this power looks: where the Lamb speaks for God, the beasts speak against God; where the Lamb rises from the dead to give life to others, the beast rises from its mortal wound only to take life. Where the Lamb goes out to conquer evil, the beast goes out to conquer the saints (Rev 13:7). Here are two utterly opposed approaches to power and judgment.

The fact that Christ is the judge of all the earth is not evidence of a vicious and unpleasant side to his character, finally showing itself at the end. It is no cause to make us waver in our love to him. Quite the opposite. The earth-shaking power of the Lamb does not mean that the humble friend of sinners has changed in his character; it is rather that his cause, his character, his light *is victorious.* His truth will drive out lies; his beauty, ugliness; his goodness, evil. The Lamb wins.

The Family of the Firstborn

In that day we will at last attain the goal of our salvation: we will be *with* him, and we will be *like* him. Those who have delighted themselves in the Lord will have, unhampered, the desires of their hearts.

For now, our "bodies are members of Christ himself" and "temple[s] of the Holy Spirit" (1 Cor 6:15, 19). Body and soul we belong to our faithful Savior, and that gives us wonderful comfort. But what polluted, inadequate temples we are! Weak, decaying, confused and sinful. We are no longer *slaves* to sin, to be sure, but it still lingers: chafing, cramping, leeching our joy and freedom. Sin steals, death bereaves, our bodies hurt, evil oppresses. That is how it is today. Yet in *that* day we will be freed at last from the very presence of sin, death and evil. The Spirit's work now of perfecting and beautifying us—of making us like Christ—will then be fulfilled. Having been elected, called, justified and sanctified in Christ, we will finally and fully share his own glorification.

You simply couldn't have a vision of hope more different from that sneaking suspicion many Christians have, that eternal life will mean being *less* truly human, having slightly less fun and somehow being less alive. Now and for eternity, becoming more like Christ means becoming *more* human, not less. Created in the image of God, we will be what we were meant to be, unshriveled, unbent and unfurled.

That means hope for our bodies, and especially sweet news for the sick, the handicapped and those in pain. As old Job cried out from all his suffering,

I know that my redeemer lives,
    and that in the end he will stand on the earth.
And after my skin has been destroyed,
    yet in my flesh I will see God;

I myself will see him
with my own eyes—I, and not another.
How my heart yearns within me! (Job 19:25-27)

For just as Christ was physically raised from the grave as the first-fruits of new life, so will we be. We will be "united with him in a resurrection like his" (Rom 6:5), our bodies freed like his from the last effects of the fall. Now blemished, sagging, aching, dying; at his appearance our bodies will transform to be perfect, splendid, glorious, powerful and imperishable. *Like his.* "Our citizenship is in heaven. And we eagerly await a Savior from there, the Lord Jesus Christ, who, by the power that enables him to bring everything under his control, will transform our lowly bodies *so that they will be like his glorious body*" (Phil 3:20-21). Then, when not just our souls but our bodies have been redeemed, we will fully share in *his* life, *his* reign and *his* victory over death (1 Cor 15:35-58).

Here is a hope that is easy to dissect and analyze. You can look at the resurrection of our bodies, at our liberation from sin and death—and it is good to stare long and hard at these things!—but it is all too easy then to lose just what makes this hope so intensely and luminously glorious. More than anything else, improving everything else, our hope is to be *with Christ.* Job longed for new flesh *in which he would see God.* And our hope is to be *like Christ.* Like him in his beautiful character, like him in his glorious resurrection body, like him in his beloved status before the Father. No eternal life and no paradise could satisfy the hearts and minds of those who know Jesus if it meant we could not have him and be like him. Every part of the Christian hope glows brighter when it is held close to him.

The Renewal of All Things

The return of Jesus will not just bring about the complete beautification and glorification of the bodies and souls of the children of God. More. Much more:

LIGHTS OF THE WORLD

That great theologian of joy, Jonathan Edwards, believed that God had designed the stars in the sky to be a picture in creation of God's people, the saints. That might look rather wacky at first glance, but the more references to stars Edwards found in Scripture, the more the connection lit up. In Genesis 15:5, the Lord took Abram outside and said, "Look up at the sky and count the stars—if indeed you can count them." Then he said to him, "So shall your offspring be." Abram's offspring, the children of his faith, would be like the stars. That was mostly about the sheer number of descendants Abram would have, of course (Gen 22:17). They would be a countless host, held in the hand of the Lord (Rev 1:16), each known by name (Ps 147:4).

But there was more: the Old Testament would go on to describe the stars as a heavenly army, a counterpart to the army of God's people on earth (Josh 5:14; Judg 5:20). Shining in the darkness, filling heaven. Paul wanted his beloved Philippians to be "children of God without fault in a warped and crooked generation. Then you will shine among them like stars in the sky" (Phil 2:15).

Today we flicker or blaze as lights in the darkness. And when he returns? Daniel 12:1-3:

> At that time Michael, the great prince who protects your people, will arise. There will be a time of distress such as has not happened from the beginning of nations until then. But at that time your people—everyone whose name is found written in the book—will be delivered. Multitudes who sleep in the dust of the earth will awake: some to everlasting life, others to shame and everlasting contempt. Those who are wise will shine like the brightness of the heavens, and those who lead many to righteousness, *like the stars for ever and ever.*

On that day we will be like the Light of the world: free at last of all darkness, surging with the light of life, radiant with love and glory.

The creation waits in eager expectation for the children of God to be revealed. For the creation was subjected to frustration, not by its own choice, but by the will of the one who subjected it, in hope that *the creation itself will be liberated from its bondage to decay and brought into the freedom and glory of the children of God.* (Rom 8:19-21)

It will be as it was in the beginning: God sent forth his powerful Word and through him brought all things into being. So it will be once again: God will utter his Word and the whole cosmos will be renewed. The creation that is sliding back into willful darkness will be suffused with the bright glory of Christ, and it will share the liberation of the children of God. The heavens and the earth will be restored and revived. The one through whom all things were made, and in whom all things now hold together, will undo all chaos, mending and binding his original handiwork back together. Jesus called it "the renewal of all things, when the Son of Man sits on his glorious throne" (Mt 19:28); Paul called it the day when God would "bring all things in heaven and on earth together under one head, even Christ" (Eph 1:10 NIV 1984).

Under *one head*, under *a ruling man*: it makes you think of Adam, when he was told: "fill the earth and subdue it. Rule over the fish of the sea and the birds in the sky and over every living creature that moves on the ground" (Gen 1:28). That first man was created head over all things. Everything was put under the feet of the man, and before he and everything under him fell, there was universal peace and harmony. Now, with that in the rearview mirror, read Daniel 7:

I looked, and there before me was one like a *son* of man, coming with the clouds of heaven. He approached the Ancient of Days and was led into his presence. He was given authority, glory and sovereign power; all nations and peoples of every language worshiped him. His dominion is an everlasting dominion that will not pass away, and his kingdom is one that will never be destroyed. (Dan 7:13-14)

When a *son* of man is led to the very throne of God and everything placed beneath his feet, we feel a delicious flutter of cosmic excitement, for we know what it must mean: all the peace and harmony, the untainted beauty of Genesis 1, blossoming afresh. The sound of weeping will no longer be heard, the lion will lie down with the lamb, the desert will bloom like the rose, the ploughman will overtake the reaper, and the mountains run with new wine. A man—this time a *faithful* man, at peace with the Ancient of Days—reigning once more in paradise. Only, unlike Adam, the Son of Man has a worship-inspiring rule that will *never* fall or be destroyed.

Isaac Watts expressed it with a bounce in his toe-tapping classic of a hymn "Joy to the World":

Joy to the world, the Lord is come!
Let earth receive her King;
Let every heart prepare Him room,
And Heaven and nature sing.

Joy to the earth, the Savior reigns!
Let men their songs employ;
While fields and floods, rocks, hills and plains
Repeat the sounding joy.

No more let sins and sorrows grow,
Nor thorns infest the ground;
He comes to make His blessings flow
Far as the curse is found.

And how far is that? In Genesis 3, the curse that followed sin meant great pain in childbirth, marital difficulties, painful labor, an earth filled with thorns and thistles. He comes to make his blessings flow into *all* those pains. Upending the fall, the Son of Man mends *all* that Adam broke.

But is this hope too good to be realistic? Can we have confidence in it? There is no obvious indication in the world around us that this is going to happen. As the years roll on, the world doesn't seem to be getting any more peaceful or unspoiled. But Christian confidence does not come from looking at the state of the world; it comes from Jesus. The ever-faithful God of truth has promised, and "no matter how many promises God has made, they are 'Yes' in Christ" (2 Cor 1:20). And more, in fact, than any promise: this new creation *has already begun*. Raised from death to new life, he is the firstborn, the firstfruit, the head of the new creation. His resurrection has started an irreversible tide.

Paradise Regained . . . and Improved

But I have been far too restrained. I have used words like *restoration* and *mending*, and they could suggest a hope that is *simply* a going back, a return to Eden. That, of course, would be paradise and enough to make anyone salivate. *But Jesus is better than Adam.* As there was more glory in the days of Solomon than in the days of his father, David, so there will be more glory in the days of the Son of Man than ever there had been in the days of the first man. For as the Last Adam is so much superior to the first, so must his reign be.

It was good before Adam fell, completely good. But he was only a creature, not a true son. He was fallible. He had only what Paul called a "natural body" (1 Cor 15:44). There was a tree to avoid and the threat of a serpent. With Christ we have so much more. We are the adopted sons of God, sharing the Son's beloved and loving life. He is infallibly faithful. He now has a glorious, imperishable body that has defeated death. Paul called it a "spiritual body" (1 Cor 15:44), the sort we will also have. And when he appears there will be no threats left and only the tree of life. With Christ we have a hope that outstrips Eden itself.

We see a little picture of this in the book of Job. In the beginning, Job lives in harmony with God and in fertile splendor, thousands of animals under his charge. "He was the greatest man among all the people of *the East*" (Job 1:3). It is all spookily similar to Genesis 2, where "the LORD God had planted a garden *in the east*" (Gen 2:8) for Adam to enjoy. Then, just as in Genesis, so in Job: Satan slithers into the scene and sees to it that Job's paradise is lost. Of course, there are all sorts of differences between Genesis and Job. That part of Genesis is concerned with the origin of sin and death; Job is concerned with suffering. But the similarity is worth spotting, for it sets us up to see that in some ways Job's personal story is also the story of humanity: from idyll to a world of suffering.

Job and His Daughters by William Blake, 1805

With that, look at the end of Job (what James 5:11 calls, literally, "the *end/goal/purpose* of the Lord"). There, Satan lies defeated in his attempts to turn Job against God, and Job—described as the Lord's faithful suffering servant (Job 42:7-8)—is given "*twice as much as he had before*" (Job 42:10). Where in the beginning Job had seven thousand sheep, in the end he has fourteen thousand sheep; where he had three thousand camels, he has six thousand camels; his five hundred yoke of oxen and five hundred donkeys become a thousand yoke of oxen and a thousand donkeys. His family doubles in size as he receives another seven sons and three daughters (the three daughters becoming the most beautiful in all the land). Where the normal length of our days is seventy years (Ps 90:10), Job gets a 140.

That festive scene at the end of Job allows us to savor something of the superabundant richness of *the* end, when Satan is defeated and the Last Man enters into the fullness of his inheritance. It is a time of double portions, of blessing upon blessing. In Deuteronomy 21:17, we read that a *double portion* is the right of the firstborn—and it is precisely *that* right that is given to the children of God, the co-heirs of Christ. So the servant of the Lord announces in Isaiah:

> The Spirit of the Sovereign LORD is on me,
>> because the LORD has anointed me
>> to proclaim good news to the poor. . . .
> Instead of your shame
>> you will receive *a double portion*,
> and instead of disgrace
>> you will rejoice in your inheritance.
> And so you will inherit *a double portion* in your land,
>> and everlasting joy will be yours. (Is 61:1, 7)

The everlasting joy and portion of the Firstborn: that is our coming inheritance!

Christ Behind Me, Christ Before Me

We children of God, then, are like seeds in the Firstfruit, and glee-fully find ourselves entirely—past, present and future—compassed about by Christ:

Past: Having died with him, we can look no further back into our past than him. Christ, not failure, is our history.

Present: United to him, we now share his glad life and standing before the Father. Filled with his Spirit, we are made ever more like him.

Future: The judge of all the earth is our faithful Savior; when he appears we will be with him, we will be like him and we will be co-heirs with him.

What, then, shall we say in response to these things? If God is for us, who can be against us? . . . For I am convinced that

neither death nor life, neither angels nor demons, neither the
present nor the future, nor any powers, neither height nor
depth, nor anything else in all creation, will be able to separate us from the love of God that is in Christ Jesus our Lord.
(Rom 8:31, 38-39)

No Other Name
Under Heaven

What do you most *enjoy* about the gospel? There are so many answers you could give, of course: guilt drowned in the blood of Christ, free salvation, the hope of the new creation, death defeated and all tears wiped away. All indescribably precious and all absolutely true. But the apostle Paul spoke of a deeper treasure, one which does not trivialize any of those great blessings of the gospel, but which stands above and before them as the wellspring of them all. He described his message as "the gospel that displays *the glory of Christ*" (2 Cor 4:4). For Paul, the gospel could not be about anything else first. It could not be about forgiveness first or justification first, for what is the point of being forgiven and justified? Not simply that we might stand forgiven and righteous in heaven. We are forgiven *in order to know and enjoy Christ*. Knowing him is the only true life.

Look how Paul phrased it: he wrote of "the gospel that displays *the glory* of Christ." For, through the gospel, the Spirit has opened our eyes to see, not merely that Christ is *true*, but more: that Christ is *glorious*. Precious, desirable, captivating, satisfying, delightful. Joy always comes through encountering beauty, and in Christ is found the highest beauty. We see *"God's glory* displayed in the face of Christ" (2 Cor 4:6). He, therefore, is our greatest treasure: the treasure of the

Father shared with us. We cannot assume or move on from him.

And we cannot *confuse* him with any other. The more you see of Jesus, the more you see he is glorious, and the more you see he is *incomparable*. He himself said, "I am the way and the truth and the life. No one comes to the Father except through me" (Jn 14:6). That could sound unnecessarily tribal or snobbish but for this: there is no one else who offers what he offers. Some religions offer paradise or nirvana; he shares with us *himself*, his very sonship, his life before the Father. If the gospel was about God sharing with us some *thing* other than himself, then Jesus' words *would* sound cliquey. Why couldn't others be purveyors of that *thing*? But since the blessing he brings *is* himself and his own life, it is plain nonsense to think of him as just one religious stall, much the same as others. Others can offer "God" or "salvation," but only when someone offers Jesus do they offer the same thing as the gospel.

He is not one way to heaven among others, and for Christians he is not one mere topic among others. Christian life and Christian theology must begin and end with Jesus Christ, our Savior and our Goal. In the luscious words of John Calvin:

> We see that our whole salvation and all its parts are comprehended in Christ [Acts 4:12]. We should therefore take care not to derive the least portion of it from anywhere else. If we seek salvation, we are taught by the very name of Jesus that it is "of him" [1 Cor 1:30]. If we seek any other gifts of the Spirit, they will be found in his anointing. If we seek strength, it lies in his dominion; if purity, in his conception; if gentleness, it appears in his birth. For by his birth he was made like us in all respects [Heb 2:17] that he might learn to feel our pain [cf. Heb 5:2]. If we seek redemption, it lies in his passion; if acquittal, in his condemnation; if remission of the curse, in his cross [Gal 3:13]; if satisfaction, in his sacrifice; if purification, in his blood; if reconciliation, in his descent into hell; if mortification of the

flesh, in his tomb; if newness of life, in his resurrection; if immortality, in the same; if inheritance of the Heavenly Kingdom, in his entrance into heaven; if protection, if security, if abundant supply of all blessings, in his Kingdom; if untroubled expectation of judgement, in the power given to him to judge. In short, since rich store of every kind of good abounds in him, let us drink our fill from this fountain, and from no other.[1]

Indeed and amen, John! Since rich store of every kind of good abounds in him, let us drink our fill from this fountain, and from no other.

Jesus did many other things as well. If every one of them were written down, I suppose that even the whole world would not have room for the books that would be written.

JOHN 21:25

Notes

Introduction: Christianity *Is* Christ

[1]John Calvin, *Commentary on Philippians, Colossians, and Thessalonians* (1844–1856; repr., Grand Rapids: Baker, 1993), Col 1:12.

[2]Andrew Bonar, *Memoir and Remains of the Rev. Robert Murray M'Cheyne* (Edinburgh: William Oliphant, 1864), p. 257.

Chapter 1: In the Beginning

[1]Thomas F. Torrance, "The Christ Who Loves Us," in *A Passion for Christ: The Vision That Ignites Ministry* (Eugene, OR: Wipf & Stock, 2010), p. 17.

[2]Stephen Charnock, *The Complete Works of Stephen Charnock* (Edinburgh: James Nichol, 1865), 4:91.

[3]Ibid., 4:163.

[4]Martin Luther, *Luther's Large Catechism* (St. Louis, MO: Concordia Publishing, 1978), p. 77.

[5]Richard Sibbes, *The Works of Richard Sibbes* (Edinburgh: James Nichol, 1862), 2:230.

[6]P. G. Wodehouse, *Summer Lightning* (London: Herbert Jenkins, 1929), p. 7.

[7]Athanasius, *Against the Arians* 3.67; emphasis mine.

[8]All emphases in biblical quotations are mine throughout.

[9]Samuel Rutherford to Lady Kenmure, November 22, 1636, *Letters of Samuel Rutherford* (Edinburgh: Banner of Truth, 1973), p. 43.

[10]Michael Reeves, *Delighting in the Trinity* (Downers Grove, IL: InterVarsity Press, 2012), p. 16; emphasis added.

[11]See p. 10 of this book; emphasis added.

[12]Jonathan Edwards, *The Works of Jonathan Edwards* (New Haven, CT: Yale University Press, 2006), 25:187.

[13]Ibid., 11:152.

[14]Ibid., 11:64.

[15]Ibid., 11:93.

[16]Martin Luther, *Luther's Works* (St. Louis, MO: Concordia Publications, 1958), 1:74.

[17]John Bradford, *The Writings of John Bradford* (Cambridge: Cambridge University Press, 1848), 1:230-42.

[18]C. S. Lewis, *Reflections on the Psalms* (London: Bles, 1958), p. 32; emphasis mine.

[19]Ibid., p. 89.

[20]G. K. Chesterton, *The Everlasting Man* (London: Hodder & Stoughton, 1925), p. 248.

[21]John Calvin, *Commentary on John* (1847; repr., Grand Rapids: Baker, 1993), 5:23; and John Calvin, *Institutes of the Christian Religion*, trans. F. L. Battles (Philadelphia: Westminster Press, 1960), 2.6.2-3; see also 4.8.5.

[22]Edwards, *Works of Jonathan Edwards*, 9:197-98.

Chapter 2: Behold the Man!

[1]John Calvin, *Commentary on Genesis* (1847; repr., Grand Rapids: Baker, 1993), 2:21.

[2]Matthew Henry, *Commentary on the Whole Bible* (1706), Gen 2:21-25.

[3]Martin Luther, *Luther's Works* (St. Louis, MO: Concordia Publishing, 1960), 35:119; emphasis mine.

[4]Gregory of Nazianzus, Epistle 101, *Nicene and Post-Nicene Fathers*, 2nd series (Peabody, MA: Hendrickson, 1996), 7:438.

[5]Theodore of Mopsuestia, *On the Incarnation* 2.291, trans. H. B. Swete, *Minor Epistles of St. Paul* (Cambridge, UK: Cambridge University Press); emphasis mine.

[6]Robert Law, *The Emotions of Jesus* (New York: Charles Scribner's, 1915), pp. 4-5.

Chapter 3: There and Back Again

[1]Richard Sibbes, *The Works of Richard Sibbes* (Edinburgh: James Nichol, 1862), 2:231.

[2]Trans. by George Papadeas, in *Greek Orthodox Holy Week and Easter Services* (Daytona Beach, FL: Patmos Press, 2007), p. 322.

[3]Thomas F. Torrance, *Incarnation: The Person and Life of Christ*, ed. Robert T. Walker (Downers Grove, IL: IVP Academic, 2008), p. 150.

[4]Martin Luther, "To Jerome Weller, July 1530," in *Luther: Letters of Spiritual Counsel*, ed. T. G. Tappert, Library of Christian Classics (Vancouver: Regent College, 2003), pp. 86-87.

[5]J. R. R. Tolkien, "To Christopher Tolkien," in *The Letters of J. R. R. Tolkien*, ed. Christopher Tolkien and Humphrey Carpenter (London: Allen & Unwin, 1981), Letter 89; emphasis mine.

[6]G. K. Chesterton, *The Everlasting Man* (San Francisco: Ignatius Press, 1993), p. 213.

[7]John Calvin, *Institutes of the Christian Religion,* trans. F. L. Battles (Philadelphia: Westminster Press, 1960), 3.11.23.

[8]Ibid., 3.11.10.

[9]Martin Luther, *The Freedom of a Christian,* in *Luther's Works* vol. 31 (Philadelphia: Fortress Press, 1957), p. 352.

[10]Edward Fisher, *The Marrow of Modern Divinity* (Ross-shire, UK: Christian Focus, 2009), p. 166; emphasis mine.

[11]Sibbes, *Works of Richard Sibbes*, 2:147.

[12]John Owen, *The Works of John Owen,* ed. William H. Goold (1826; repr., Edinburgh: Banner of Truth, 1965), 1:238.

[13]Gerrit Scott Dawson, *Jesus Ascended* (New York: T & T Clark, 2004), p. 7.

[14]G. F. Barbour, *The Life of Alexander Whyte* (London: Hodder & Stoughton, 1925), p. 82; P. T. Forsyth, *The Principle of Authority* (London: Independent Press, 1913), p. 273.

[15]Thomas Goodwin, *The Works of Thomas Goodwin* (Edinburgh: James Nichol, 1862), 4:149.

[16]Ibid., 4:87.

[17]Ibid., 2:lxxiv-lxxv.

[18]Charitie Bancroft, "The Advocate" (1863).

Chapter 4: Life in Christ

[1]John Calvin, *Commentary on 1 Corinthians* (1844; repr., Grand Rapids: Baker, 1993), 1:9.

[2]John Calvin, *Commentary on John* (1847; repr., Grand Rapids: Baker, 1993), 6:26.

[3]Martin Luther, *Luther's Works* (St. Louis, MO: Concordia Publishing, 1957), 31:298.

[4]Charles H. Spurgeon, "The First Sermon in the Tabernacle," *Metropolitan Tabernacle Pulpit* (1861; repr., Pasadena, TX: Pilgrim Publications, 1986), 7.169.

[5]Charles H. Spurgeon, "The Statute of David for the Sharing of the Spoil," *Metropolitan Tabernacle Pulpit* (1891; repr., Edinburgh: Banner of Truth, 1970), 37.323-24.

[6]Richard Sibbes, *The Works of Richard Sibbes* (Edinburgh: James Nichol, 1862), 2:34; emphasis mine.

[7]John Calvin, *Institutes of the Christian Religion*, trans. F. L. Battles (Philadelphia: Westminster, 1960), 1.1.2.

[8]Charles Spurgeon, *Christ's Glorious Achievements* (Carlisle, PA: Banner of Truth, 2014), pp. 94-95; emphasis mine.

[9]John Owen, *The Works of John Owen*, ed. William H. Goold (1826; repr., Edinburgh: Banner of Truth, 1965), 1:395.

[10]Ibid., 1:279.

Chapter 5: Come, Lord Jesus!

[1]Heidelberg Catechism, Question 52; emphasis mine.

[2]Martin Luther, *D. Martin Luthers Werke*, Kritische Gesamtausgabe (Weimar: Herman Böhlau, 1920), 53:401.

Conclusion: No Other Name Under Heaven

[1]John Calvin, *Institutes of the Christian Religion*, trans. F. L. Battles (Philadelphia: Westminster, 1960), 2.16.19.

Image Credits

Chapter 1: In the Beginning

Christ as the true Word, the true Manna, the true blossoming staff,
Speculum Humanae Salvationis, c. 1360: Wikimedia Commons,
http://commons.wikimedia.org/wiki/File:Speculum_Darmstadt
_2505_20v.jpg.

Nick and Arius, from the Nicene fresco in the Monastery of Soumela,
Turkey: This is a faithful representation of a piece of artwork not in
copyright, and therefore is in the public domain.

The Heavenly Rose, by Gustave Doré: Wikimedia Commons, http://
commons.wikimedia.org/wiki/File:Paradiso_Canto_31.jpg.

"Each arrow overshot his head," by Elmer Boyd Smith: Wikimedia
Commons, http://en.wikipedia.org/wiki/File:Each_arrow_overshot
_his_head_by_Elmer_Boyd_Smith.jpg.

Christ as the Glory of the Lord in Ezekiel 1, by Lucas Cranach the
Younger, Wittenberg Bible, 1541: Scan from the author's library.

Albani-Psalter: Ausweisung aus dem Paradies, ca. 1130: Wikimedia
Commons, http://en.wikipedia.org/wiki/File:Albani-Psalter_Aus
weisung_aus_dem_Paradies.jpg.

Chapter 2: Behold the Man!

The Body of Abel Found by Adam and Eve, by William Blake: Wikimedia Commons, http://en.wikipedia.org/wiki/File:Blake-Abel.jpg.

Adam Comes to Eden—mosaic in Monreale Cathedra: Photo by
Sibeaster, Wikimedia Commons, http://commons.wikimedia.org
/wiki/File:Adam_comes_to_Eden.jpg.

Schedelsche Weltchronik, by Hartmann Schedel: Wikimedia Commons,
http://commons.wikimedia.org/wiki/File:Schedelsche
_Weltchronik_d_010.jpg.

Schädel Adams am Berge Golgatha, by Fra Angelico, 1435: Wikimedia
Commons, http://en.wikipedia.org/wiki/File:Fra_Angelico_090.jpg.
Saint Irenaeus (c. 130-202): Wikimedia Commons, http://en.wiki
pedia.org/wiki/File:Saint_Irenaeus.jpg.
The Annunciation, by Fra Angelico, 1430–1432: Wikimedia Commons,
http://commons.wikimedia.org/wiki/File:La_Anunciación,_by_Fra
_Angelico,_from_Prado_in_Google_Earth_-_main_panel.jpg.
The Storm on the Sea of Galilee, by Rembrandt, 1633: Wikimedia
Commons, http://en.wikipedia.org/wiki/File:Rembrandt_Christ_
in_the_Storm_on_the_Lake_of_Galilee.jpg.
Marriage at Cana, Originally from Niels Hemmingsen: *Postil, 1576:*
Wikimedia Commons, http://commons.wikimedia.org/wiki/
File:H.P._Hansen_pg136_Marriage_at_Cana.jpg.

Chapter 3: There and Back Again
The Crucifixion, by Lucas Cranach the Elder, 1502: Wikimedia
Commons, http://commons.wikimedia.org/wiki/File:Lucas_Cranach_
the_Elder_-_The_Crucifixion_-_Google_Art_Project_(520041).jpg
Christ in the Sepulchre, Guarded by Angels, by William Blake: Wiki-
media Commons, http://commons.wikimedia.org/wiki/File:William
Blake-_Christ_in_the_Sepulchre,_Guarded_by_Angels.jpg.
"His burden fell off his back," Illustrations by Frederick Barnard, J.D.
Linton, W. Small, etc., 1890: Wikimedia Commons, http://commons
.wikimedia.org/wiki/File:PProg_17_p47_HisBurdenFellOffHisBack
.jpg.
Der Auferstandene 1558, by Lucas Cranach: Wikimedia Commons,
http://en.wikipedia.org/wiki/File:Der-Auferstandene_1558.jpg.
Isaac Blessing Jacob, by Gerrit Willemsz Horst: Wikimedia Commons,
http://en.wikipedia.org/wiki/File:Horst,_Gerrit_Willemsz._-_Isaac
_blessing_Jacob_-_Google_Art_Project.jpg.
The Return of the Prodigal Son, by Pompeo Batoni, 1773: Wikimedia
Commons, http://en.wikipedia.org/wiki/File:Pompeo_Batoni_003.jpg.
The Ascension of Christ, by Dosso Dossi: Wikimedia Commons, http://
en.wikipedia.org/wiki/File:Dosso_Dossi_022.jpg.

Melchizedek offering bread and wine, from a sixth-century mosaic in Sant'Apollinare in Classe, Ravenna: Wikimedia Commons, http://commons.wikimedia.org/wiki/category:Melchizedek#mediaviewer/File:Sacrific_classe.jpg.

Chapter 4: Life in Christ

Woodcut for "Die Bibel in Bildern," by Julius Schnorr von Carolsfeld, 1860: Wikimedia Commons, http://commons.wikimedia.org/wiki/File:Schnorr_von_Carolsfeld_Bibel_in_Bildern_1860_226.png.

From Spurgeon's Sermons Fifth Series; Sheldon & Co. 1858; At Surrey Music Hall, Kennington: Wikimedia Commons, http://en.wikipedia.org/wiki/File:SpurgeonSurrey.jpg.

Return of the Spies from the Land of Promise, as in Numbers 13, engraving by Gustave Doré: Wikimedia Commons, http://commons.wikimedia.org/wiki/File:Dore_Return_of_the_Spies_From_the_Land_of_Promise.jpg.

Way to Calvary, back panel of the *Maestà* altarpiece, Cathedral of Siena Duomo, by Duccio: Wikimedia Commons, http://commons.wikimedia.org/wiki/File:Bearing_of_the_Cross_(Duccio_di_Buoninsegna).jpg.

Woodcut for "Die Bibel in Bildern," by Julius Schnorr von Carolsfeld, 1860: Wikimedia Commons, http://commons.wikimedia.org/wiki/File:Schnorr_von_Carolsfeld_Bibel_in_Bildern_1860_194.png.

Chapter 5: Come, Lord Jesus!

The Revelation of St John: 13. The Adoration of the Lamb and the Hymn of the Chosen, by Albrecht Dürer: Wikimedia Commons, http://commons.wikimedia.org/wiki/File:Durer,_apocalisse,_13_adorazione_dell%27agnello_e_canto_degli_eletti.jpg.

Saint-Michel emblème de Bruxelles: Wikimedia Commons, http://commons.wikimedia.org/wiki/File:Saint_Michel_emblème_de_Bruxelles.jpg.

Job and His Daughters, by William Blake: Wikimedia Commons, http://en.wikipedia.org/wiki/File:Job_and_His_Daughters_Butts_set.jpg.

Scripture Index

OLD TESTAMENT

Genesis
1, *13, 29, 41, 55, 116*
1:11-12, *41*
1:26, *29*
1:27, *36*
1:28, *36, 81, 115*
2, *37, 38, 44, 117*
2:1, *26*
2:8, *118*
2:10, *73*
2:21-22, *37*
2:23, *43*
3, *44, 72, 116*
3:15, *43, 96*
3:20, *43*
3:21, *66*
3:23-24, *73*
4, *45*
5, *39*
5:3, *18, 39*
14, *41, 42*
15:1, *21*
15:5, *114*
15:19, *90*
16:10-13, *30*
18:1-8, *31*
19:24, *31*
22:17, *114*
27, *66*
27:27, *66*
32:24-30, *31*
32:30, *29*
48:15-16, *30*

Exodus
3:2-15, *30*
16:10, *30*
23:19, *74*
24:10, *29*
24:10-11, *31*
25:40, *77*

28:36, *77*
33:11, *29*

Leviticus
9:23, *30*
16, *77*
16:2, *14, 32*
18:25, *109*
25:8-10, *105*
26:12, *107*

Numbers
13:6, *90*
13:23, *91*
32:12, *90*

Deuteronomy
18:15, *56*
21:17, *119*

Joshua
5:14, *114*
15:13, *91*

Judges
2:1, *30*
5:20, *114*
13:20, *32*
13:22, *29*
19, *38*
19:25, *38*

1 Samuel
2:25, *32*
4:4, *14*
24:13, *40*

1 Kings
7–8, *76*

Job
1:3, *117*

16:19-21, *79*
16:20-21, *32*
19:25-27, *113*
42:7-8, *118*
42:10, *118*

Psalms
1, *56*
2:6, *76*
8:4-8, *81*
14:1, *26*
15:1, *73*
15:2-5, *73*
16:8-11, *74*
22:22, *93*
24:7-10, *80*
33:6, *56*
45:2, *57*
45:6, *57*
45:7, *56*
90:10, *118*
98:4-9, *109*
102:25, *24*
107:20, *13*
107:29, *50*
110:1, *79*
110:4, *80*
113:6, *33*
147:4, *114*

Proverbs
3:11-12, *94*
8:30, *95*
12:4, *70*

Song of Solomon
8:5, *68*

Isaiah
6:5, *29*
7:14, *32, 46*
8:17, *93*

38:4, *13*
42:1, *18*
52:13-14, *58*
53:4-5, *58*
54:5, *68*
61, *55*
61:1, *119*
61:1-2, *92*
61:7, *119*
62, *69*
62:3-5, *70*
62:5, *31*
63:9, *31*

Ezekiel
1, *29*
3:23, *30*
16, *68*
28:13-14, *73*
37:27, *107*

Daniel
3:25, *31*
7, *115*
7:13-14, *115*
12:1-3, *114*

Amos
3:1, *13*

Zechariah
2:8-9, *31*

Malachi
2:16, *85*
3:1, *33*

APOCRYPHA

2 Esdras
7:118, *39*

NEW TESTAMENT

Matthew
3:17, *18*
4:6, *51*
5:3, *51*
5:9, *18*
10:7, *51*
11:12, *89*
11:27-30, *21*
12:28, *51, 56*
13:17, *50*
14:29-30, *101*
16:16, *51*
18:4, *51*
19:28, *115*
22:36-37, *86*
26:30, *93*

Mark
14:36, *71*
14:61-62, *51*
15:39, *51, 59*

Luke
1:35, *46, 55*
1:76-79, *52*
2:25-35, *33*
2:49, *51*
3:21-22, *51*
3:38, *36*
4:18-19, *55, 92*
6:35-36, *18*
9:28-36, *51*
22:19, *84*
23:42, *15*
24:39, *72*
24:51, *72*

John
1:1, *13*
1:3, *24*
1:4, *48*
1:4-5, *35*
1:5, *110*
1:13, *56*
1:14, *14*
1:17, *14*
1:18, *29, 30*
1:49, *56*
2:4, *44*
2:16-17, *52*
2:21, *51*

3:6, *45, 46*
3:17, *20*
4:34, *52, 90*
5:23, *11*
5:38, *99*
5:39, *99*
5:40, *99*
6:37, *100*
6:39-40, *99*
8:39, *18*
8:58, *31*
10:17, *59*
10:28, *99*
10:30, *14*
12:32, *60, 81*
14:6, *122*
14:9, *14*
14:19, *67*
14:20, *84*
14:23, *84*
14:27-28, *83*
14:31, *37*
15:1-8, *98*
15:2, *99*
17:24, *18*
19:19, *59*
19:26, *44*
20:31, *50*
21:25, *124*

Acts
1:11, *106*
4:12, *122*
5, *95*
9:4, *98*
10:38, *56*
13:32-34, *19*
13:33, *19*

Romans
1:4, *19, 64*
3:26, *60*
4:25, *65*
5:5, *90*
5:12, *39*
5:14, *36*
5:15, *39*
5:17, *45*
5:17-19, *39*
6:2, *92*
6:3, *61*
6:5, *113*

8, *71*
8:3, *20*
8:11, *56*
8:14, *71*
8:14-15, *90*
8:15, *71*
8:19-21, *115*
8:21, *65, 108*
8:31, *120*
8:34, *79*
8:38-39, *120*
15:9, *93*
16:20, *96*

1 Corinthians
1:18-31, *60*
1:30, *66, 122*
6:15, *112*
6:19, *112*
8:6, *24*
15, *40*
15:20-23, *40*
15:35-58, *113*
15:44, *117*
15:45, *36*
15:45-49, *56*
15:52, *106*
16:22, *108*

2 Corinthians
1:20, *117*
3:18, *11, 102*
4:4, *35, 121*
4:6, *85, 110, 121*
4:8-10, *97*
5:21, *65*
6:16, *107*

Galatians
2:20, *62*
3:13, *122*
3:26-27, *70*
4:4, *20*
4:6, *71*
6:14-15, *62*

Ephesians
1:6, *18*
1:10, *115*
2:15-18, *84*
4:10, *81*
5:32, *38*

Philippians
1:21, *9*
1:23, *85*
2:7, *33*
2:15, *114*
3:8, *9*
3:20-21, *113*

Colossians
1:6, *81*
1:15, *24, 35*
1:16, *18*
1:17-18, *24*
1:18, *65, 108*
2:12, *61*
3:1-4, *6*

1 Thessalonians
1:10, *108*
4:16, *106*

1 Timothy
3:16, *64, 100*

2 Timothy
4:7, *99*

Titus
2:11-12, *103*
2:13, *108*

Hebrews
1:3, *14*
1:5, *19, 70*
1:8-9, *57*
1:10, *24*
2, *93*
2:11, *93*
2:12, *93*
2:13, *93*
2:14, *47*
2:17, *122*
4:14, *56*
4:14-16, *75*
5:2, *75, 122*
7:10, *41*
7:25, *79*
8:5, *77*
9:11, *77*
9:14, *56*
9:24, *77*
10:12, *77*

12:2, *95*
12:5-6, *94*
13:9, *10*

James
5:11, *118*

1 Peter
4:12-13, *94*

1 John
2:22-23, *49*
3:2, *102, 108*
3:16, *60*
4:19, *89*
5:13, *100*

2 John
7, *47*

Jude
5, *31*

Revelation
1:16, *114*
3:14, *14*
5:9, *110*
12:4, *111*
12:11, *111*
13, *111*

13:2, *111*
13:3, *111*
13:7, *111*
13:11, *111*
19:7, *68, 107*
21:2, *37*
21:3, *107*
22:5, *110*
22:17, *107*
22:20, *108*

Finding the Textbook You Need

The IVP Academic Textbook Selector
is an online tool for instantly finding the IVP books
suitable for over 250 courses across 24 disciplines.

ivpacademic.com